Demons, Lies & Shadows

D1453116

In friendship,

Pierre Gilbert

Demons, Lies & Shadows

A PLEA FOR A RETURN TO TEXT AND REASON

By Pierre Gilbert

Winnipeg, Manitoba   KINDRED PRODUCTIONS   Hillsboro, Kansas

Published simultaneously by Kindred Productions, Winnipeg, Manitoba R3M 3Z6 and Kindred Productions, Hillsboro, Kansas 67063

Cover Design: Mario Buscio

Layout: Audrey Plew

Library and Archives Canada Cataloguing in Publication
Gilbert, Pierre, 1959-
  Demons, lies and shadows : a plea for a return to text and reason / Pierre Gilbert.
Includes bibliographical references and index.
ISBN 978-1-894791-17-5
  1. Spiritual warfare. 2. Demonology. I. Title.
BV4509.5.G477 2007   235'.4   C2007-906666-6

Printed in Canada

Table of Contents

Acknowledgments

The publication of a book requires a lot of time, much effort and the support of many friends. This one was no exception. I cannot do justice to all the people who have had some part in making this project a reality, but I would like to publicly acknowledge some of them.

I am deeply grateful to the Canadian Mennonite University and the Mennonite Brethren Biblical Seminary for providing over the years the resources needed to complete this book. Many thanks also to Kindred Productions for their willingness to risk publishing a book on a topic that is not as "hot" as it used to be, but still represents an area of great need today.

A special word of thanks to Sandy Smith for enthusiastically sharing her editorial and biblical expertise.

Finally, I wish to express my appreciation to my wife Monika and my adult children, Rachel, Pierre James and Steven for being so gracious in sharing me with my scholarly endeavors and for their willingness to engage in both polite conversation and lively debate whenever I needed to test some ideas.

Finally, I would like to express my gratitude to Norma and Jean Marot, who, many years ago, taught me the value of community and the importance of truth. To them, I owe a debt of gratitude that I will never be able to repay.

Introduction

The Devil Among Us?

A book about demons in 2007?!? Surely there must be some kind of mistake here. Is there still anyone out there who seriously believes in Satan, demons and other assorted spiritual entities? Might as well write a letter to Santa Claus, or look for the magical wardrobe to Narnia. If there ever were such things as spiritual beings—good or evil—surely they were swept away with the millennium bug!

I fear it may not be quite that simple. In fact, I have an uneasy feeling that belief in demons, spiritual beings or magic is not simply a faint memory from the dark ages, now superseded by the joyful laughter of enlightened children of the 21st century. I am not sure that a significant number of people would openly admit to believing in demonic beings, yet there is little doubt that a broad segment of the population cultivates sustained interest in related matters.

For starters, consider the data from a few simple searches on *Google*: Voodoo: 11,100,000 results! Thousands of sites offering every conceivable spell to improve our lives: love spells, money spells, career spells, good luck spells, protection spells, etc., etc.

Black magic: 8,210,000 results!! Again, an endless number of sites where anyone with a valid credit card number can access the "powers of darkness."

New Age: 136,000,000 results!!! Thousands of websites promising eager seekers the keys that unlock the secrets of the universe.

Internet searches on Satan, the devil or demons admittedly do not yield as many pages. But a search on the occult delivers 6,420,000 results and uncovers many thousands of links dealing with every imaginable related subject: tarot card reading, witchcraft, runes, numerology, Satanism and the like.

All this may seem harmless to some. I submit it is anything but. Firstly, this renewed interest in the occult and magic is just plain puzzling. Why would any person who has experienced first-hand the endless benefits of modern-day science turn to ancient belief systems that flatly contradict the most assured results of empirical research? The fact that so many people are belies a kind of ideological confusion that is beyond comprehension. Secondly, the money involved is staggering. The New York State Protection Board recently reported that just for psychic lines, the Psychic Friends

Network brings in as much as $400 million annually.[1]

What does this all have to do with demons? As we well know, labels don't always reflect the true contents of the box. We may not publicly acknowledge the existence of Satan and the demonic, or seriously label anything as such; yet other dimensions of North American life suggest otherwise.

Consider, for example, the furious proliferation of Internet pornography. Can anybody seriously believe that thousands of women willingly and joyfully choose a life of heart-wrenching humiliation? The sheer unimaginable scale of it all is astonishing.

Consider the heartless trafficking of women and children. Accurate numbers are hard to come by, but even the lowest estimates represent a staggering reality. In 2002, Richard Re, a senior editor of the Harvard International Review wrote: "Conservative estimates indicate that at least 27 million people, in places as diverse as Nigeria, Indonesia and Brazil, live in conditions of forced bondage. Some sources believe the actual figures are 10 times as large."[2] It is often reported that North America represents the largest market for these defenseless human beings. While I certainly puzzle at the cruelty of the vile profiteers who deal in human flesh, there would be no large-scale outlet for their depraved souls were it not for the demand that fuels the trade.

Finally, consider the thousands upon thousands of people who promote and participate in endless types of deviant sexual practices. The issue for me is not so much that they participate in these practices, but that we have stopped calling them deviant. That some people engage in various bizarre sexual acts is one thing, and frankly of little immediate concern to me. But it is another issue altogether to suggest, as is increasingly becoming the case, that sex a la carte is an appropriate organizing principle for society.

The Supreme Court of Canada recently ruled in favor of decriminalizing swinger clubs. At first glance that seems innocuous enough. As stated

---

1 Matt Bean, "Seeing the Future—or Just Dollar Signs," Court TV.com, http://www.courttv.com/news/feature/misscleo_ctv.html (accessed January 5, 2006).

2 Richard Re, "A Persisting Evil," *Environment*, vol. 23 (2002), http://hir.harvard.edu/articles/951/1/ (accessed January 20, 2006).

in a CNN article: "Newspaper editorialists fumed in Toronto but largely yawned in Montreal."[3] Signs of an underworked court perhaps? What do I know? Maybe the State has no business dictating which sexual acts are legitimate and which are not. The major issue in this case is not so much the legalization of these establishments, but the basis upon which the decision was made. In what amounts to a redefinition of decency, the courts decided that harm, rather than community standards, would constitute the basis upon which legality would be defined.

Again, at first glance, that seems reasonable enough. But let's spin this out a little to see what it really means. If we say that a certain type of activity is not illegal because it entails no obvious harm to anyone, are we then saying that swapping sexual partners is no more innocuous than, say, scratching an itch? If such practices are not inherently harmful, are we then saying they may in fact be inherently good? Perhaps even virtuous? A lifestyle worthy of the highest praise? While I seldom debate an issue on the basis of the "slippery slope" argument, I find myself wondering if there is any slope left at all! Sounds more like a jump without a parachute to me. I see no end to the social chaos that will eventually emerge out of this new moral paradigm.

Finally on the topic of sex, let me add one more thing: Sex is everywhere! There is more sex in our environment than sugar in our food. Yet never has so much sex given birth to so few children. Western societies, Europeans and Canadians more so than the Americans, are copulating into oblivion. As the columnist Mark Steyn describes it, the "cult of non-procreative self-gratification" is as unsustainable as they come, yet we are more passionate about the fate of polar bears—which incidentally are doing just fine in the global warming environment—than about the catastrophic consequences of low birth rates on the most extraordinary civilization ever to grace this planet. The Western world is enthusiastically turning itself into a giant geriatric ward while we hear nothing from our fearless political and intellectual elites.

---

3 CNN.com, "Newspaper editorialists fumed in Toronto but largely yawned in Montreal," http://www.cnn.com/2005/WORLD/americas/12/26/canada.swingers.reut/ (accessed January 2, 2006).

While there is no shortage of good things happening around us, we must admit there is also something sinister and deadly at work in our world. Europe, the birthplace of Western civilization and for centuries the center of some of the world's greatest cultural accomplishments, has been the theater of some of the worst atrocities ever perpetrated in human history, including two world wars and the chilling murder of six million Jews. The Soviet Union was home to an economic system that promised heaven on earth to all, yet it saw 40 million dead at the hands of a single mad man: Stalin. And what can we make of an ideology that promises paradise to those who murder Muslims and non-Muslims alike in the defense of the faith?

Maybe the devil does not exist and demons are but shadows under our beds. No doubt humans have it within themselves to indulge in the worst of evils. And yet, I believe there is more.

From time immemorial, human beings have held fast to a belief that spiritual entities exist and interact with them for good or evil. The Yanomamö—people living in the Amazon rainforest completely isolated from Western civilization and virtually unknown until the early 1960s—developed their whole culture around spirit worship.[4] Either such spiritual beings exist or they don't. If the notion of a Satan and demons is just some 4000-year-old misunderstanding, then I apologize for burdening the world with yet another deluded book on demonic powers. If, on the other hand, such evil entities do exist, then we need to know more about them.

I personally believe in the existence of disembodied beings whose only purpose is to poison the lives of men and women. My goal for this book is to provide a new understanding of what they are, how they relate to us, and what to do about them. This book is for clergy who want to get their hands on a biblical theology of demonism, for committed laypeople who want to be better informed, and for missionaries who struggle with how to share the message of Jesus Christ in cultures that are often saturated with superstitious beliefs.

---

4 Mark Ritchie provides a vivid eye-witness account of life amongst the Yanomamö in *Spirit of the Rainforest*, 2nd ed. (Chicago, IL: Island Lake Press, 2000 [1996]).

The Church Tackles Demons

Throughout its history, the Church has vigorously believed that malevolent beings conspire against God and humans alike to bring about death and chaos. Since the beginning of the early Church, Christians have taught that the world is immersed in a spiritual struggle involving evil entities bent on the corruption and, ultimately, the destruction of humanity. Through the centuries, Christians have actively opposed demonic forces through public prayer and exorcisms.[5]

Although the Church never actually ceased its campaign against demonic powers, there has been, at least in the last four decades, a remarkable renewal of interest in this area. Until about 1960, the concept that is now broadly known as *spiritual warfare*[6] was mostly identified with the Pentecostal movement. But then the phenomenon of spiritual warfare gained increasing acceptance in the broader evangelical community: first through the charismatic renewal in the early 1960s and then through what is commonly known as the Third Wave Movement.

A number of key Christian leaders and authors have especially influenced and advanced the Movement: C. Peter Wagner, Fuller Theological Seminary's School of World Mission; Tom White, founder of Mantle of Praise Ministries (now Frontline Ministries); John Dawson, Southwest U.S. Director of Youth With A Mission; and Frank Peretti, author of the popular novels *This Present Darkness* (1986) and *Piercing the Darkness* (1989). In fact, much of the theology generally identified with spiritual warfare and the Third Wave Movement was in great part popularized, at least in North America, by Peretti's novels describing the fate of men and women caught in epic battles between demonic forces and angelic warriors, a theme also recently developed in the *Left Behind* series.

The teachings of the spiritual warfare movement are now found across the entire spectrum of Christian denominations and para-church

---

5 For a helpful historical survey of such practices, see Gerald Ediger, "Strategic-Level Spiritual Warfare in Historical Perspective," *Direction 29* (2000):125-141. See also Jeffrey Burton Russell, *Mephistopheles: The Devil in the Modern World* (Ithaca, NY: Cornell University Press, 1986), 91.

6 According to Ediger, the expression, "spiritual warfare," was first formally used in print by Michael Harper, a leader of the British charismatic renewal, who wrote a book by the same title (see *Spiritual Warfare* [London: Hodder and Stoughton, 1970]).

organizations. This is not to say that all the proponents of spiritual warfare adhere to exactly the same beliefs. While there are indeed variations, as evidenced in the controversy surrounding the concept of "territorial spirits,"[7] yet surprisingly, there has also been broad acceptance of the Third Wave Movement's core beliefs, at least in the way it portrays the relationship between the human and demonic spheres.

Demonic Warfare Today!

I would like to clarify the terminology I use. Although the expression "spiritual warfare" is often understood as the dealings between Christians and demonic forces, the term also sometimes refers more broadly to the whole area of Christian spirituality and the practice of the spiritual disciplines. This book is not about the spiritual disciplines. My primary purpose is to address the demonic and to describe as accurately as possible how the relationship between humans and demons is defined within the framework of biblical theology. To minimize any confusion, I will most often use the term "demonic warfare" rather than "spiritual warfare" to describe the object of this study.

Most proponents of demonic warfare share a common set of beliefs about how demons interact with human beings. Let me summarize the most basic teachings.

- People can be possessed (or demonized) by evil spirits with or without their consent.

- Some Christians have a special gift in discerning and exorcizing a demonic presence.

- There are "territorial spirits" who hold a special kind of domination over neighborhoods, cities and even countries.

- Some Christians have a special ability in identifying and challenging a territorial spirit's control.

- Objects or places can project evil influences and act as conduits for demonic oppression.

- Traumatic events, either in our lives or in our ancestral past, can make us particularly vulnerable to demonic influence.

---

7 See particularly Clinton Arnold, *Powers of Darkness, Principalities and Powers in Paul's Letters* (Downers Grove, IL.: InterVarsity, 1992); *Three Crucial Questions about Spiritual Warfare* (Grand Rapids, MI: Baker, 1997).

How Do We Really Know?

Most of the readers are likely familiar with all or some of these teachings. And based on the many conversations I have had over the years, I suspect that even conservative Christians accept these affirmations at face value. But ultimately, how can we really know if these beliefs are true or false?

When it comes to understanding the spiritual world, one of the obvious problems—particularly as it relates to the relationship between evil spirits, magic and the occult—is the utter opacity of the demonic. By this I mean our inability to assess the spiritual world directly and empirically. It would be very helpful if we could entice the devil or some of his demons to appear at a study conference; and ask them questions about their origin, purpose, nature and their interaction with human beings. Maybe we could trick them into entering a test tube to determine at what temperature they boil and freeze. Psychologists could study their behavior alone and in groups. What great fun that would be! But sadly, it is not that simple. I suspect demonic beings do not have real substance; they cannot be caught with a *Ghost Busters* style spiritual vacuum cleaner.

Obviously, we must use another source of information to construct a portrait of the devil and demonic beings. Spiritual warfare specialists tend to base much of their understanding of demons on stories gleaned either from their own experience or that of others. When I refer to such anecdotes, it will not be to prove a thesis but rather to illustrate how demonic warfare is generally understood today.

Considering the difficulties intrinsic to the study of demons, it is absolutely imperative that we build our understanding of satanic beings and the nature of their interaction with humans from a careful investigation of the only assured source of data we have: the Bible.

One of the issues we face when talking about the devil is the question of whether he exists at all. Those who hold firmly to a secular worldview do not, by definition, acquiesce to the objective existence of evil beings or an overarching devil who is bent on promoting evil in the world. Academics most often define the devil either in psychological terms as a projection of human evil or a symbolic force, or in anthropological terms as the expression of a primitive worldview.[8] For true secularists, even the mere suggestion that there might be some reality undergirding the notion of demons is inadmissible. To admit the existence of a personal being like Satan would lead to their worldview's utter collapse. Just as a secular worldview denies the existence of God, it must also deny the existence of the devil.

So then, to answer the question of whether or not the devil exits really depends on one's worldview. As a Christian, I view the Bible—both the Old and the New Testaments—as divinely inspired. I believe these texts, interpreted in due respect for their literary genres and their historical specificity, are foundational to a worldview that reflects ultimate reality. To state that the Bible is inspired is essentially to believe that it presents a true window into the fundamental nature of reality. Though there are but a few ambiguous references to the devil and demons in the Old Testament,[9] the New Testament offers plenty of evidence to support the reality of these malevolent beings.

Can demons really influence humans? If so, how?

In this book, I will endeavor to answer a number of questions about the demonic and related subjects like the occult, the New Age and magic. Can we come under demonic influence by playing certain computer games or watching television programs that use occult images and practices? Can Satan or demons take control of human beings without their consent? Can demons occupy objects and inhabit certain places? If the devil has been vanquished, why is he still active? Is there any reality behind voodoo or other occult practices? Do we need people with special gifts to protect us from the influence of the devil and evil spirits? What is the real nature of spiritual warfare? Do we need protection from curses? Can demons legitimately gain strongholds in our lives? Is there any reality to magic and

---

8   Russell discusses the shift from belief in the devil as an objective reality to that of a psychological construct in *Mephistopheles*, see particularly, pp. 262-264.

9   In the annex, I briefly comment on each one of the passages dealing with Satan in the Old Testament. For more details, on Satan in the Old Testament, see Sydney H. T. Page, *Powers of Evil* (Grand Rapids, MI.: Baker, 1995), 11-42.

occult powers? Can people really have psychic powers? Can we know the future? Can we communicate with the dead? Are we the powerless victims of anonymous and overpowering forces that shape our future and destiny? All these questions point to one question: Can demons really influence humans, and if so, how?

The debate surrounding spiritual/demonic warfare goes far beyond whether a person, Christian or not, can be demon-possessed. As the questions listed above suggest, they also relate to our perception of God, of free will, and of the very nature of reality. I would even suggest that what is at stake is our very understanding of evil and how we manage it in daily life.

To think of the demonic as a fringe phenomenon of little interest is to make a grave mistake. Spiritual warfare conferences are constantly being held in North and Latin America. Christian parents are increasingly concerned about the spiritual impact non-Christian worldviews taught in the schools will have on their children. Extending far beyond the classroom, parents are increasingly concerned about their kids being exposed to a popular culture which continues to show a remarkable hunger for the New Age and the occult.

In the movie, *End of Days*, Arnold Schwarzenegger plays a washed out police officer who must battle the devil to avoid 1000 years of demonic rule over the world. In *Buffy the Vampire Slayer* and its spin-off *Angel*, the main heroes spend the better part of the weekly one-hour shows battling beings that appear to come from the very pit of hell itself. Computer games commonly use demonic themes. The player in *Doom* plays a stranded space marine who must destroy the devil. Demonic symbols like the pentagram and the inverted cross appear in the game. There are numerous pentagrams in *Quake*, a game similar to *Doom*. Pentagram symbols are also found in *Warcraft 2* and *Duke Nukem 3D*. The game *Diablo* contains explicit occult themes. The player's character combats "Diablo" (Satan), along with demonic and magical monsters. Although the player portrays the "good guy," he must use magic spells and potions and read occult books and scrolls to fight the hellish monsters. He must also supernaturally heal himself of the many wounds he receives. Much of the same could be said about *Mortal Kombat, Final Fantasy, Dungeons and Dragons*, etc. While it may be argued that the game encourages spiritual warfare and Christianity's opposition of demonic forces, the game actually teaches players to fight evil through occult practices. Such games do not simply introduce kids to the occult, they actually gradually draw them into a worldview that intrinsically contradicts the modern scientific worldview.

Are Christians justified in being concerned about these things, or are they overreacting? My intent is to provide some concrete answers to these troubling questions.

The Roadmap

In the first chapter, rather than focusing on various details of the demonic warfare position, I will seek to describe more broadly the worldview that emerges in popular demonic warfare writings. Focusing on worldview will allow us to go beyond simple particularities and will help us to identify some of the major assumptions spiritual warfare writers commonly hold. It will also enable us to systematically describe the most popular perceptions of demonic warfare. Finally, it will provide a model that can be more easily compared and evaluated.

In the second chapter, I will articulate the basic outline of a biblical worldview by examining chapters 1 to 3 of the book of Genesis. Since these chapters represent the theological foundation of the entire Bible, they must therefore be given precedence in developing a biblical worldview.

In the third chapter, I will examine the New Testament's portrayal of the demonic by focusing particularly on the Gospel of Mark and 1 Corinthians.

In the last chapter, I will address some of the concrete questions and issues that are most prominently linked to demonic warfare.

One day, as Satan was taking a stroll on the highway to hell, he asked a few of his minions: "What are men saying about me these days?" They said: "Here Dark Lord, take this book. You can read all about it in the first chapter."

Chapter 1:

Understanding Demonic Warfare Today. An Issue of Worldview

Introduction
Why is the devil so hard to figure out?

There are basically three reasons. First, we simply have no direct way to question the devil about his activities! Aside from many people's reluctance or even refusal to believe the devil exists, there is no way to measure, quantify or qualify satanic activity in the world.

Second, much of what is said about the demonic is drawn from personal experience, dramatic anecdotes, traditions, legends and popular culture. In Christian circles, the popular perception of the devil and his activities has been effectively shaped by Frank Peretti's *This Present Darkness*, a novel about a terrifying demonic plot to take over a small college town. More recently, the *Left Behind* series co-authored by Tim LaHaye and Jerry Jenkins describes how a man named Nicolae Carpathia, who in reality is the Antichrist, rises to world power after the Rapture to unleash satanic forces upon the world. As in Peretti's novels, LaHaye and Jenkins portray Satan and his minions with extraordinary supernatural powers they use to thwart God's purposes. Mainstream culture's perception of Satan and demons as overwhelmingly powerful entities has been shaped by Hollywood's relentless flow of horror and action movies. Typical of Hollywood fare is the action movie, *End of Days*, in which Arnold Schwarzenegger plays a washed up ex-cop who becomes embroiled in a fight against Satan's demonic plot to impregnate a woman and trigger an endless age of darkness on the earth.

Much of what we think we know comes from sources that are essentially unverifiable. As much as Christians may profess that the Bible is a reliable source of information on spiritual matters, much of what is written about Satan and the demonic only loosely reflects the biblical material.[1] My personal assessment of spiritual warfare literature is that too much of it is seen through a grid that values personal experiences and anecdotes over the biblical text. Thus, the age-old question can be asked again: Do we interpret the Bible in light of our experience or do we interpret our experience in light of the Bible? Third, many people experience frustration

---

1 A notable exception to this general rule is Page's book, *Powers of Evil*. In his study of the demonic in the Bible, Page provides a very careful exegetical analysis of the Old and New Testament passages that pertain to the devil and demons.

as they attempt to evaluate the popular model of demonic warfare because they fail to view it from a broader theoretical perspective. It is not sufficient to assess specific practices or beliefs without including a careful treatment of the underlying worldview.

Although there are various models of spiritual/demonic warfare, as David Powlison points out,[2] we have witnessed the emergence of one basic approach in the last 20-25 years that appears to span the entire spectrum of the Charismatic Movement, the Third Wave Movement and the other evangelical traditions.

This is not to suggest that there is unanimity on all aspects of demonic warfare theology.[3] As Powlison aptly conveys: "Although there is intramural skirmishing on secondary matters, they are close enough in their distinctive emphases to be considered one movement."[4] The emergence of the Third Wave Movement has doubtless been the major catalyst behind the evangelical world's renewed interest in spiritual warfare and deliverance. Since not everyone is familiar with the Third Wave Movement, a brief description by Thomas H. McAlpine will serve us well.

> The name [Third Wave] was coined by C. Peter Wagner. It recognizes three major movements of the Holy Spirit in [the last] century: the classic Pentecostal movement at the beginning of the century, the charismatic renewal movement of the '60s and '70s, and the evangelical discovery of spiritual gifts in the '80s. The "third wave" affirms its links with the previous waves, but distinguishes itself from them in that it does not promote a single "baptism in the Spirit" and does not give special status to the gift of tongues. For this reason, the third wave group does not describe itself as "charismatic" or "pentecostal."[5]

---

2 See David Powlison, *Power Encounters. Reclaiming Spiritual Warfare* (Grand Rapids, MI: Baker, 1995), 32-34.

3 The main point of contention is whether there is any legitimacy to the belief that there are territorial spirits that can be engaged in the spiritual sphere. For example, while C. Peter Wagner wrote extensively about the reality of territorial spirits and the strategy to overcome their destructive influence (see *Engaging the Enemy. How to Defeat Territorial Spirits* [Ventura, CA: Regal, 1991], Clinton Arnold forcefully challenged that view's legitimacy (see *Three Crucial Questions about Spiritual Warfare* [Grand Rapids, MI: Baker, 1997]).

4 See Powlison, *Power Encounters*, 32.

5 See Thomas H. McAlpine, *Facing the Powers: What Are the Options?* (Monrovia, CA: Marc, 1991), 5.

In his excellent survey, Thomas H. McAlpine identifies some of the most influential leaders who have not only shaped the Third Wave Movement, but the very understanding of spiritual warfare in the wider evangelical world. They are C. Peter Wagner of Fuller Theological Seminary's School of World Mission; Tom White, founder of Mantle of Praise Ministries (now Frontline Ministries); John Dawson, Southwest U.S. Director of Youth With a Mission; and Frank Peretti,[6] author of the popular novels *This Present Darkness* (1986) *and Piercing the Darkness* (1989).[7]

A Critique of Demonic Warfare Theology

Right from the outset, I need to clarify that although I am presenting how demonic warfare is now most commonly understood, I am not endorsing the model. Instead, this discussion of basic beliefs and underlying worldview will set the stage for demonstrating that the assumptions undergirding demonic warfare do not actually reflect the biblical worldview but may in fact manifest a mode of thinking in the Christian community that is becoming more and more prevalent in postmodern society. I will seek to show that the demonic warfare approach resembles a Christianized form of animism "in which spirits and magic are used to explain everything."[8]

Why a Discussion of Worldview?

There are a number of ways to examine and critique a given ideology or a theological system. In regards to demonic warfare, for example, one could examine the key biblical passages that its proponents cite most often and critically assess their scriptural interpretation. Such an evaluation does

---

6 Some may object or at least question the relevance of referring to works of fiction in the context of this study. But Frank Peretti's novels are viewed by some as more than simple fiction stories. According to Steven Lawson, an important Third Wave leader, Peretti's novels represent a dramatic depiction of the conflict Paul describes in Eph. 6:12. He writes: "These fictionalized accounts tell how packs of demons have taken over complete towns, infesting government, education, even churches. And they depict how Christians fight back with prayer and how angels clash with evil principalities" (See Steven Lawson, "Defeating Territorial Spirits," in *Engaging the Enemy* [Ventura, CA: Regal, 1991], 31).

7 For an excellent comparative survey of the various traditions pertaining to the issue of spiritual warfare, see McAlpine, *Facing the Powers*. McAlpine deals specifically with the Third Wave movement on pp. 43-56.

8 Paul Hiebert, "Excluded Middle," in *Anthropological Reflections on Missiological Issues* (Grand Rapids, MI: Baker Books, 1994), 189-201.

need to be done and I have, in fact, devoted some space in the Annex of this book to interpreting these controversial passages. But rather than focusing on various details of the demonic warfare position, I believe it is more helpful to think broadly in terms of the worldview that emerges in popular demonic warfare writings. An approach that first focuses on worldview will allow us to go beyond simple particularities and will enable us to identify some of the major fundamental assumptions that these writers hold in common about the nature of the universe, humanity and God.

As a first step, I will seek to outline the most salient elements of the demonic warfare model. This will not only enable us to describe and analyze the underlying worldview, it will also provide a theoretical model that can be used within the framework of a comparative approach. This book's primary point of reference will be the biblical worldview as defined first and foremost by the Creation account found in Genesis 1-3.

What do I mean by worldview? A worldview is a basic frame of reference that enables us to define reality and test the validity of our experience.[9] It constitutes—consciously or unconsciously—a certain perception of reality. By definition, a worldview is coherent, self-validating and self-consistent. Whether or not it truly reflects reality is quite another issue. Suffice it to say that any particular worldview is reality for those who embrace it. But worldviews are not static entities that remain forever unchanged. Under certain circumstances, people may encounter a degree of cognitive dissonance that originates from a glaring inconsistency between their experience of a new phenomenon and their conceptual frame of reference.

For example, the report of a UFO sighting over "Area 51" in Nevada would normally constitute a major dilemma for a person who doesn't believe intelligent extra-terrestrial life exists. This person will deal with the new phenomenon by maintaining the status quo, rejecting the evidence or integrating the new data.

In the first instance, the person makes no attempt at integrating the new phenomenon into his or her worldview. They will simply choose to

---

9   For a detailed definition, see James Sire, *The Universe Next Door*, 4th ed. (Downers Grove, IL: InterVarsity Press, 2004 [1988]).

live with a basic degree of cognitive dissonance. This may not be the greatest option from a mental health perspective, but for many people, it represents an adequate way of dealing with new phenomena—as long as the evidence doesn't become overwhelming.

In the second option, the validity of the phenomenon is rejected and the new data is not allowed to modify the previously-held worldview. People who adopt this strategy will systematically reject any evidence that could undermine their fundamental beliefs. Those who fit into this category are the people who claim the Apollo missions to the moon were elaborate hoaxes.

Finally, some people choose to integrate the new phenomenon into their system of beliefs. They accept the new data as real and allow it to modify their original worldview. In extreme situations, they may even embrace a radically different worldview altogether. A dramatic religious conversion would represent a good example of such a process.

Our understanding of reality is much more than a few isolated beliefs; there is always a coherent system of assumptions—a plausibility structure— that controls, organizes and monitors the flow of data our senses collect from the environment. Understanding someone else's view of reality is therefore much more than identifying a list of isolated beliefs. It is an attempt at understanding how the most basic beliefs interact together to form a dynamic conceptual system.

Demonic Warfare: A Portrait

Although there is a certain commonality among the various approaches to demonic warfare theology, it would not be accurate to suggest that there is complete unanimity on what constitutes demonic warfare. McAlpine suggests that there are four relatively well-defined paradigms of spiritual warfare.[10] However, the majority of specialists who have contributed to popularizing spiritual warfare in recent years have done so from a remarkably common perspective. Though they may not all live in the same room, it would be fair to say that they all live in the same house. In other words,

---

10 The four models are: 1) The Reformed tradition ("transformation by osmosis"); 2) The Anabaptist tradition ("over against"); 3) the Third Wave tradition ("expect a miracle"); and 4) the social science tradition ("sociological Bible").

there are variations in the way they handle specific issues related to different aspects of spiritual warfare and deliverance. But on the whole, we can safely say that the majority of writers who associate broadly with the evangelical tradition can be found at the same "address."

We can also rate the various approaches on a spectrum from extreme to middle of the road. Charismatic preachers like Don Basham and Benny Hinn can be placed to the far left, Third Wave authors like John Wimber, Peter Wagner and Charles Kraft fall more moderately on the left, whereas less extreme theologians and mainstream evangelicals like Neil Anderson, Timothy Warner, Clinton Arnold and others would be situated closer to the right side of the spectrum. Wherever we may decide to position them, the fact remains that these teachers and writers essentially share similar assumptions about the essential character of demonic warfare.

So then, let us articulate a comprehensive picture of the worldview that constitutes the underpinnings of demonic warfare theology.

Sources and Basic Assumptions

Attempting to represent a theological model can be fraught with danger. There is always the possibility of misrepresenting the approach, either by painting a caricature of it or by intentionally using inadequate sources.[11] I have attempted to avoid both trappings (usually the first is a result of the second) by using as main sources authors whose works are recognized as representative and who have significantly impacted the church community. I have also used sources that are cited by the authors themselves as descriptive of their understanding of demonic warfare. Although I will occasionally provide short critical assessments of some of the elements of the demonic warfare ideology in this chapter, I will save the more comprehensive critique of that model for the following chapter.

The book edited by C. Peter Wagner, *Engaging the Enemy*, represents a basic reference work. First, Wagner is widely recognized as a major leader in the area of demonic warfare, particularly as it pertains to evangelism. Second, Wagner himself states that his book is seminal in terms of providing

---

11 A good example of this approach can be found in *What Would You Do? A Serious Answer to a Standard Question* (Scottdale, PA: Herald, 1983), a book on pacifism edited by John H. Yoder where the only article that addresses the issue of violence from the perspective of the just war theory is at best a spindly example of it.

a basic reader for those who wish to become more familiar with the issues. Third, the book represents a major work on the issue of demonic warfare because it includes the perspectives of seventeen different authors from a variety of church traditions. I suggest that *Engaging the Enemy* represents a fair and accurate picture of how demonic warfare is most often understood in church circles today. However, I have not limited myself to this book but have consulted other works as well to gain a more complete picture of spiritual deliverance, particularly as it relates to demon and human interaction. In this last respect, I have often referred to Ed Murphy's *The Handbook for Spiritual Warfare* [12] and Fred Dickason's *Demon Possession and the Christian*,[13] two highly influential works in shaping our present understanding of spiritual warfare.

It is impossible to understand the trajectory of demonic warfare theology without grasping the importance of the following two concepts.

1. Created to Fight

Underpinning the popular demonic warfare model is the belief that the Christian life is essentially characterized by warfare. Although Wagner is careful to mention that other metaphors could be used to characterize the Christian life, he states explicitly that he is not free to do so, for "The Bible itself describes our fight against the devil as warfare. And I believe the reason for this is clear. We are in a life and death struggle."[14] The key biblical passage to justify this position is Ephesians 6:12: "*For our struggle is not against enemies of blood and flesh, but against the rulers, against the authorities, against the cosmic powers of this present darkness, against the spiritual forces of evil in the heavenly places.*"[15] Of course, the question of origins immediately comes to mind. Where do these evil beings come from and why are they allowed to poison our lives? The answer to this question is linked to humanity's very origin and derives from God's ultimate purpose for the human race. In his book, *Taking our Cities for God*, John Dawson suggests that evil and evil spirits are necessary elements in terms

---

12   Ed Murphy, *The Handbook for Spiritual Warfare* (Nashville, TN: Thomas Nelson, 1992).

13   Fred C. Dickason, *Demon Possession and The Christian: A New Perspective* (Wheaton, IL: Crossway, 1987).

14   Wagner, "*Spiritual Warfare*," in Engaging the Enemy, 4.

15   Unless otherwise noted, all Scripture references are taken from the New Revised Standard Version.

of enabling humanity to reach its full potential. The presence of these evil spirits is attributed to an angelic rebellion that occurred before the creation of the world and humanity. [16] Dawson further proposes that these rebellious angels, or at least some of them, were left free to oppose God and his kingdom to provide the necessary setting for human destiny's ultimate unfolding.

Considering the catastrophic consequences of the presence of leftover demons in the world, one might ask why they were allowed to remain on earth. That question does not escape Dawson. He writes, "Why would God do that? Why would he leave a free force in opposition to himself? I believe it is because the development of man in his ultimate potential depended on an experience with an adversary. That's right, God wanted us to fight."[17] Dawson further expands on this theme by proposing a necessary connection between the fact that humanity is created to rule and its status as a warrior race. "Man is a warrior race, made in God's own image and destined to rule beside Him."[18] The author sees proof of this in the use of the word "subdue" (Gen. 1:28) which, according to Dawson, implies an "adversarial position." [19]

One cannot overestimate the importance of this concept for Dawson; he repeatedly refers to this theme in his chapter entitled "Born to Battle."[20] The primary rationale behind this is eschatological. He writes: "This hostile environment is essential for our eternal future. Mankind has been made to take dominion. It is necessary that we face an antagonist during our brief apprenticeship to qualify in character to rule with Christ in eternity."[21]

[Alert]:
Nowhere does the creation account state or even suggest that it was necessary to place humanity within a "warfare" setting to bring about our full potential.

---

16 John Dawson, *Taking Our Cities for God. How to Break Spiritual Strongholds* (Lake Mary, FL: Creation House, 1989), 128.

17 Dawson, *Taking Our Cities for God*, 128.

18 Dawson, *Taking Our Cities for God*, 128.

19 Dawson, *Taking Our Cities for God*, 128.

20 Dawson, *Taking Our Cities for God*, 127-133.

21 Dawson, *Taking Our Cities for God*, 130.

Nor was it necessary to create certain warfare conditions so that we could develop the needed skills to rule with God in eternity. The Creation account does not describe the physical environment in which humanity is embedded as "hostile." On the contrary, the world is consistently described as "good." In my opinion, Dawson appears to confuse the so-called prerequisites for developing a warrior race with the conditions necessary to allow the emergence of free will (Gen. 2:15-17) and its meaningful expression (Gen. 2:15-17; 3:1-24; 4:1-12). God's ultimate purpose for humanity is not that we should become a "warrior" race, but that we should become a people composed of individuals who freely choose to love and serve God; a race endowed with a special kind of self-awareness that could be described as free will. The universe is first and foremost designed to facilitate that overall objective.[22] In addition, God used a clearly stated test of obedience (Gen. 2:15-17) to bring about what he intended to produce in humanity, not an occult encounter with demons.

2. In the Last Days!

The second concept to keep in mind as we try to understand demonic warfare is the urgency that many people feel is linked to the present phase of human history. According to Wagner, the end of the 20th century represents the culmination of history. He claims that we are now living in one of the most remarkable periods of history in regards to demonic activity. Not only have we entered into a period of exceptional spiritual vitality, we are also on the verge of an intense and critical manifestation of Satan. Therefore, the Church can expect to enter into a concentrated and possibly climactic period of spiritual warfare. This conviction is expressed in a number of ways.

Wagner writes:

As we begin moving into the 1990s, I sense, along with many other Christian leaders, that the Holy Spirit is saying, 'Prepare for warfare'… In 1970 we saw the first seeds of what is developing now into the greatest prayer movement in living memory. In 1980 a contemporary renewal of the prophetic ministry began and, while this is not so widely recognized as yet, the gift of prophecy and the office of prophecy and the office of prophet are reemerging. Now in 1990 spiritual warfare is moving to the forefront.[23]

---

22 C. S. Lewis in *The Problem of Pain* (New York, NY: HarperSanFrancisco, 1996 [1940]) proposes a very insightful discussion of this very question.

23 Wagner, "Spiritual Warfare," 3-4.

Steven Lawson, a journalist on the staff of *Charisma & Christian Life* magazine, adopts a similar position. He writes, "Earl Paul of Chapel Hill Harvester in Atlanta, Georgia, has said that as we enter the 1990s we embark upon the most intense time of spiritual warfare in history." [24]

Pastor Larry Lea of the Church on the Rock in Rockwall, Texas, in an article entitled "Binding the Strongman" bases his suggestion that the world is overrun by hordes of demons on Luke 11:21-23 and 11:24-26. But parallel to this phenomenon, God is also raising an army of people who "know what the score is." He writes:

> Today God is raising up a company of people who know what the score really is, where the action really is in God. They're aware that unclean spirits are roaming this earth, seeking places to dwell in order to destroy men and women. This emerging company will have listening ears for what the Holy Spirit is saying to the church today, and they'll answer His call to battle. [25]

[Alert]:

The introduction of an eschatological/end-times dimension into the discussion of demonic warfare is a very interesting development; for it ends up attributing an extraordinary degree of urgency to the issue and a correspondingly critical importance to those who are on the "front lines" of this "war." If we live in the period of time that constitutes history's climax on a cosmic scale, then spiritual warfare specialists are virtually ascribed a savior-like status. The urgency these leaders give to their cause directly results in a heightened sense of importance and authority for themselves. This gives rise to the concern that these "experts" may be—consciously or unconsciously—using tactics similar to those used by end-of-the-world cult leaders who create an atmosphere of crisis through the conviction that the world is coming to an end so that they themselves become the only ones who can save their followers. I am not suggesting that men like Peter Wagner are cult leaders bent on destroying their followers. But I think there is a real possibility that some of the individuals who adopt this perspective may be setting themselves in a position of authority over people who may be, for various reasons, particularly vulnerable to psychological or spiritual abuse.

---

24 Steven Lawson, "Defeating Territorial Spirits," 31.

25 Larry Lea, "Binding the Strong Man," in *Engaging the Enemy*, 85.

Demonic Warfare: Elements of Worldview

Demonic warfare specialists have developed a relatively clear and coherent understanding of God, humanity and the universe. The following points represent some of the major elements of the demonic warfare worldview.

Violence and Creation

Demonic warfare specialists teach that the very creation of the universe has been tainted by a cosmic conflict that occurred between God's forces and the rebellious demonic powers. Though this war actually took place before the world's creation, its effects permeate all of history. At the moment of creation, demonic forces bent on humanity's destruction already inhabited the universe. Though God's forces were victorious, the consequences of that conflict adversely affected humankind and the very environment in which we live. The practical implication of this situation is that humans were introduced into a world that was already tainted by sin, conflict and war. According to this belief, the first human beings were put into a hostile universe dominated by oppressive and destructive occult forces.[26]

Mythologization of the Universe

According to today's predominant understanding of demonic warfare, the universe is populated with millions of superhuman/supernatural beings whose only purpose is to destroy humanity and God's designs. Vernon J. Sterk speculates that the number of these demons ranges in the millions.[27] I use the expression "mythologization" to denote the belief that these beings not only inhabit the world, but also express their presence through the physical universe. This belief resembles the ancient perception of the gods and demons of Egyptian and Mesopotamian religions. The implications of this are developed under the following points.

The Universe as Subject

Within the framework of this mythologized worldview, the physical universe takes on the characteristics of consciousness in that the various elements of nature reflect a diversity of deities. Spiritual warfare specialists

---

26 This is a thesis Gregory Boyd extensively develops in his book *God at War* (Downers Grove, IL: InterVarsity Press, 1997). The chapter entitled, "Slaying Leviathan" (93-113), addresses the issue of a primordial fall and its effects on creation.

27 See Vernon J. Sterk, "Territorial Spirits and Evangelization in Hostile Environments," in *Engaging the Enemy*, 148.

teach almost universally that a person can be oppressed by demonic influence simply by coming into contact with an object or a place that has, at one time, been associated with some form of occult influence. The spiritual beings inhabiting such an object or place adversely affect the lives of humans by manipulating the physical elements of nature. Demonic warfare writers assume that the principles of magic are valid and real. Objects can have supernatural powers, the spoken word is inherently efficient, and places and objects can mediate evil powers and influence.[28]

Fred C. Dickason vividly describes the possibility of being infected by objects that have been associated in one way or another with the occult:

> The necessity of removing all practices or objects associated with demon-inspired activities is quite clear from Scripture. We have found that it is necessary to free men from the bondage of demons today as well. A woman told me that she was being molested at night by unseen hands. She mentioned that she had over the head of her bed a gift from a man who had made sexual advances toward her at her workplace. We dedicated the gift to destruction, and she removed it. The harassment ceased. A young, lady student, who was part of a Florida beach evangelism team, received a leather string bracelet from a man to whom she witnessed. He said it was a friendship bracelet. Sometime after he had tied it on her wrist, she began to have strange sensations and disorienting feelings. I suggested that this fit the pattern of a love charm and that there might be some demonic association. We prayed, I broke it off her wrist, and since that time the harassment has disappeared. God removed the demon influence.[29]

Timothy M Warner, a professor at the School of World Mission and Evangelism at Trinity Evangelical Divinity School and a specialist in the area of spiritual warfare, offers another example of the belief in the power of objects:

> For example, a young lady shared the following story with me, prefaced by the comment, "It is good to have someone to talk with about this

---

28 Sterk, "Territorial Spirits," 218. Peter Wagner devotes an entire chapter to the relationship between objects and demonic influence in "Demons behind Bushes," in *Warfare Prayer* (Ventura, CA: Regal, 1992), 73-86. Wagner also relates an incident during which he came to believe that his house in Altadena, California was inhabited by evil spirits ("The Visible and the Invisible," in *Breaking Strongholds in Your City*, ed. by C. Peter Wagner [Ventura, CA: Regal, 1993]), 62-64. See also Timothy M. Warner, *Spiritual Warfare*, (Wheaton, IL: Crossway, 1991), 94.

29 See Fred C. Dickason, *Angels, Elect and Evil* (Chicago, IL: Moody, 1975), 251.

who won't think I'm crazy." She was studying French in preparation for service in Africa. She was by nature a very energetic, outgoing person; but she had become very depressed and was having difficulty sleeping and studying. After struggling with this for awhile, a missionary with whom she had become acquainted asked her where she was staying. Upon examining her room, they discovered that the previous occupant had placed many occult objects in the room. Apparently some of the spirits associated with those objects had attached themselves to the room and its furnishings. They prayed, commanding the spirits to leave, and that night the new missionary slept normally and was able to continue her language study. [30]

These anecdotes represent fairly well the demonic warfare movement in the evangelical church today. These are not isolated cases. There are in fact hundreds of such stories that can be gleaned from literature.[31] The average demonic warfare practitioner can easily provide dozens of eye-popping reports involving the demonic.

[Alert]:
As we will see later on in this book, the New Testament writers are much more concerned about our mental and spiritual habits than about the possibility of random influence by demons (see for instance Rom. 12:1; 1 Pet. 2:4-12).

Demonic Pantheon

According to the third wave ideology, the spirit world reflects a highly sophisticated organization that includes a hierarchy of demonic beings. At the top is none other than Satan. Wagner writes: "Satan is referred to several times as the god of this age or the prince of the power of the air. He has usurped God's authority and set up his Kingdom here on earth. His power is awesome. Luther insightfully said, 'On earth is not his equal.'"[32] It's not that Satan is considered to be omnipotent. Vernon J. Sterk, a field missionary of the Reformed Church of America, suggests that Satan acts by delegating his power and authority to evil spirits whose number, he speculates, ranges in

---

30 Warner, *Spiritual Warfare*, 94.

31 Kurt Koch's books on the demonic offer a remarkable array of such stories. See in particular *Counseling and Occultism* (Grand Rapids, MI: Kregel, 1972); *Demonology: Past and Present* (Grand Rapids, MI: Kregel, 1973); and *Occult ABC* (Grand Rapids, MI: Kregel, 1981).

32 Wagner, "Spiritual Warfare," 5

the millions.[33] One of the main agendas of these beings is to intervene in the human sphere to obstruct Christians from discerning God's will.[34]

Although most authors do not provide a detailed organizational structure of the demonic world, it is said to be characterized by a hierarchy of evil spirits organized according to rank. Three major categories of demons are identified: territorial spirits, middle-level spirits, and ground-level spirits. The extent of the spirit's power is directly proportional to its rank; the higher the rank, the more powerful that spirit is and the more spiritual power is needed to deal with it.[35] These spirits are said to have specific names[36] and well-delineated roles and territories.[37] In some cases, however, the evil spirits hold generic names that mostly reflect their sphere of action. Larry Lea refers to spirits of accusation, abuse, drunkenness, fornication, greed, homosexuality, lust, prostitution, sex, vice, destruction, dissent, aggressiveness, violence, war, etc.[38] Regardless of rank, these spirits manifest specific characteristics which are reflected in the territories or individual people under their control.

Attempting to document the existence of territorial demons and their influence over specific regions, Vernon J. Sterk describes the interesting belief system of the Tzotzil tribes with whom he worked for 20 years. These tribes can identify both good and evil spirits. For example, the J'ic'aletic or 'Blackmen' are "looters and rapists who commit indiscriminate attacks of all kinds of evil."[39] These spirits exhibit clearly specialized roles while still having territorial designations and assignments. The power of these spirits

---

33 Vernon J. Sterk, "Territorial Spirits," 148.

34 Wagner,, "Spiritual Warfare," 17.

35 See Fred C. Dickason, *Angels, Elect and Evil* (Chicago, IL: Moody, 1975), 251 and Wagner, "Spiritual Warfare," 17.

36 For instance, according to Wagner, the Latin American Christian psychologist Rita Cazebas has discovered that there are six worldwide principalities under Satan, named (allowing that this was done in Spanish) Damian, Asmodeo, Menguelesh, Arios, Beelzebub and Nosferasteus. She reports six governors under each who have authority over each nation. For example, those over Costa Rica are Shiebo, Quiebo, Ameneo, Mephistopheles, Nostradamus and Azazel. Those over the U.S.A. are Ralphes, Anoritho, Mancester, Apolion, Deviltook and one which is unnamed (C. Peter Wagner, "Territorial Spirits," in *Wrestling with Dark Angels*, ed. By C. Peter Wagner and F. Douglas Pennoyer [Ventura, CA: Regal, 1990], 84). See Also Wagner, "Territorial Spirits," in *Engaging the Enemy*, 48.

37 For an extensive treatment of this issue, see John Dawson, *Taking Our Cities for God. How to Break Spiritual Strongholds* (Lake Mary FL: Creation House, 1989).

38 See Larry Lea, "Binding the Strongman," 83-95.

39 Vernon J. Sterk, "Territorial Spirits and Evangelization in Hostile Environments," in *Engaging the Enemy*, 149.

is limited to a specific geographical area. A number of strategies emerge in dealing with these spirits. For example, since the Tzotzil believe they do not benefit from the protection of their guardian spirits, some tribal people will avoid entering a territory that is outside their tribal boundaries. On the other hand, sick people who have the opportunity to go to an evangelical Christian who lives outside the tribal territory will choose to remain at the Christian's house until they are completely well, thus confirming the belief that the spirit's evil influence outside its traditional territory is limited.[40] If a person inadvertently carries a spirit, the Christian casts it out and commands it to return to where it came from.

Sterk is careful, however, to point out that the reality of spiritual territoriality is not limited to the Tzotzil tribes or to our own times. He notes that this phenomenon has been observed in other parts of the world. For instance, in the 1800s, John Nevius relates the case of a wealthy family who was allegedly financially ruined by a local spirit in Ho-kia-chwang, China.[41]

The notion of territorial spirits is a major component of spiritual warfare. Confronting spirits that hold cities or whole regions captive is perceived as a necessary prerequisite to any evangelistic endeavor. John Dawson[42] and Peter Wagner[43] have been most influential in articulating a theology of demonic territoriality. Although the concept of demonic territoriality has occasionally been critiqued by scholars,[44] spiritual warfare practitioners mostly agree on its legitimacy. More recently, this dimension of spiritual warfare has come to be known as "strategic level spiritual warfare" (SLSW).[45]

---

40 See Vernon J. Sterk, "Territorial Spirits and Evangelization in Hostile Environments," 149-151.

41 Vernon J. Sterk, "Territorial Spirits and Evangelization," in *Engaging the Enemy*, 151. The existence of the territorial model is also confirmed by anthropologist Jacob Loewen, Mennonite Brethren missionary in "Which God Do Missionaries Preach?" in *Engaging the Enemy*, 165-175.

42 Note particularly John Dawson, *Taking Our Cities for God.*

43 In addition to some of the extensive material on territorial spirits provided in the book *Engaging the Enemy* (see, for instance, Steven Lawson, "Defeating Territorial Spirits"; C. Peter Wagner, "Territorial Spirits"; Timothy M. Warner, "Dealing with Territorial Demons"; Jack Hayford, "Possessing our Cities and Towns"; John Dawson, "Seventh Time Around: Breaking Through a City's Invisible Barriers to the Gospel"; Vernon J. Sterk, "Territorial Spirits and Evangelization"; etc.), C. Peter Wagner has also edited what amounts to a manual on territorial spirits and spiritual mapping: *Breaking Strongholds in Your City* (Ventura, CA: Regal Books, 1993).

44 See, for instance, Clinton Arnold, *Powers of Darkness. Principalities and Powers in Paul's Letters* (Downers Grove, IL: InterVarsity Press, 1992); *Three Crucial Questions about Spiritual Warfare* (Grand Rapids, MI: Baker, 1997).

45 Gerald Ediger provides an excellent historical retrospective of SLSW in "Strategic-Level Spiritual Warfare in Historical Retrospect," *Direction*, vol. 29 (2000):125-141. For a detailed treatment of SLSW, see Peter Wagner, *Praying with Power* (Ventura, CA.: Regal Books, 1997).

The Christian Experience is Characterized by War

Since this approach proposes the model of warfare as the operative principle of human existence, it is important to realize that the conditions usually associated with war are said to characterize human life in general and the Christian experience in particular. The Christian is described as living under conditions of war and is therefore under the constant threat of being attacked and overcome by evil spirits. The more effective a Christian leader is, the greater the likelihood that evil forces will target that person. The Christian must expect and will experience intense spiritual conflict.

Demonic warfare specialists trace the reality and intensity of the spiritual warfare that our world is experiencing to Jesus' invasion of Satan's kingdom. When Jesus came to earth, he broke the power of Satan through his death and resurrection. But as Wagner points out, although Satan has certainly lost the war, this "invasion" triggered a ferocious resistance by Satan, resulting in violence and warfare on a cosmic scale. "He is not taking this invasion lying down. That is why violence had erupted both in the heavenlies and here on earth." [46]

[Alert]:
The New Testament speaks of Christ breaking the powers of darkness (John 12:31; Col. 1:13; 2:14-16; 2 Pet. 2:4; Heb. 2:14; Rev. 12:11). Yet Wagner and others suggest that the intensity of demonic manifestations have in fact increased since Christ's coming.

Gregory A. Boyd eloquently supports the view that humanity is embroiled in a cosmic spiritual war in his book, *God at War.* For Boyd, the reality of a spiritual war that directly affects the earth and humanity is foundational to the biblical worldview. This insight is not unique to Scripture. According to Boyd, the idea of a terrible conflict on a different sphere of existence is universally recognized and can be found in mythologies all over the world and throughout history. This warfare worldview is a key component in explaining the existence of evil on the earth. While he is careful not to deny human freedom and responsibility, Boyd nevertheless states that much of the evil that has plagued human history can be attributed to this other war. He quite rightly points out that human history is filled with countless examples

---

46 Wagner, "Spiritual Warfare," 5.

of men and women committing evil actions. Whether or not human history is mostly characterized by evil, as he suggests,[47] its reality is an undeniable fact of human existence. Boyd suggests the only way to account for this horrific reality is to appeal to a spiritual war involving supernatural beings. He writes:

> If the earth has indeed been besieged by a controlling diabolical force (Satan) who commands legions of hostile demons…, then but only then, it is not surprising that we see around us "more signs of the demonic than of the true God," as König says. Then, and only then, are we not surprised to find that in this war-torn land, "there is more pain and misery, injustice and violence…than love, prosperity, justice and joy," as König further observed.
>
> For this is exactly what war looks like. If we grant the intelligibility of the war itself, there is simply no further problem in intellectually understanding why any particular atrocities occur. In a state of war, bullets fly, bombs explode, mines are stepped on, and children are maimed. War is hell. This is to be expected. [48]

A little further on, he adds: "This depth of horror, this scope of barbarism, these authors contend, cannot be explained on strictly naturalistic terms. It can be rendered intelligible—in the type of perverse intelligibility such events are capable of—only by the category of the demonic."[49]

The Christian Experience is Characterized by Fear and Uncertainty

The source of spiritual attacks is manifold and is ultimately impossible to identify with precision. Any negative feeling or emotion can be evidence of demonization. Coming into contact with a demon-possessed person, contacting an occult object, or being present in a place inhabited by or associated with evil spirits can all bring an individual under demonic influence. The extent of the fear—if not the terror—and the uncertainty inherent to the Third Wave ideology is particularly evident in Frank Peretti's novels, which take the basic teachings of the major demonic warfare leaders to their logical conclusions. Not everyone who believes in spiritual warfare will experience

---

47 See also A. König, *Here Am I: A Believer's Reflection on God* (Grand Rapids, MI: Eerdmans, 1982), 20.

48 Boyd, *God at War*, 59.

49 Boyd, *God at War*, 70.

this kind of uncontrollable fear. I am, however, suggesting that anyone who fully integrates the spiritual warfare worldview will increasingly experience fear and paranoia.

In *Taking our Cities for God*, Dawson provides a series of incidents to illustrate the ominous character of the demonic as demons manifest their influence in human affairs.[50] On one occasion, Dawson was being picked up by his wife and his three sons at the Los Angeles Airport. As soon as he entered the car, he immediately knew there was something wrong: "As soon as the door opened, I sensed it. I felt the oppression of an evil spirit right in the van with my wife and three sons—not possessing anybody, just lurking in the background."[51] On another occasion, when board members were expressing doubts about the financial viability of Youth With a Mission, he sensed there was a spirit of unbelief in the boardroom. According to Dawson, Satan is a religious spirit who targets religious leaders and institutions; his main weapons are accusation and deception. The more influential the leader or the organization, the more active Satan will be: "I think he's probably trying to accuse and deceive the Christian leader who is most threatening to his kingdom."[52]

Part of the reason behind the inherent uncertainty of the demonic warfare worldview lies in its dualistic understanding of the universe. Demonic warfare specialists maintain that the real struggle is not in the physical realm, but lies "above." The evil we observe results from war in the spiritual realm. "According to the Bible our lives are lived in the midst of an invisible spiritual war …The fact is, there is a battle raging over your city and it is affecting you right now."[53] "Physical violence represents an encroachment of spiritual violence into the material realm."[54]

This model functions in both directions. If incidents of violence in the visible world reflect conflicts in the spiritual sphere, conversely, any real social progress will only be possible if the spiritual realm has been conquered first. "…remember that positive political reformation will only grow out of territory gained in the unseen realm."[55] For example, Dawson recognizes

---

50   Dawson, *Taking Our Cities for God*, 24-25.

51   Dawson, *Taking Our Cities for God*, 24.

52   Dawson, *Taking Our Cities for God*, 24-25.

53   Dawson, *Taking Our Cities for God*, 27.

54   John Dawson, *Taking Our Cities for God*, 152.

55   Dawson, *Taking Our Cities for God*, 153.

the sociological factors that contribute to the decay of a neighborhood like his own in Los Angeles. In fact, his book, *Taking our Cities for God*, represents a decent introduction to urban studies. But ultimately, he claims, these deplorable conditions exist because of the spirits that hover over the neighborhood: "Spirits of despair, hopelessness, depression, discouragement and rejection torment this community."[56]

Whereas many Third Wave proponents focus on the territorial demons affecting cities and neighborhoods, authors such as Rodger K. Bufford, Ed Murphy and Charles Kraft have written quite extensively on the relationship between individuals and demonic beings.

In a book dealing with counseling and the demonic, Bufford states that a person can come under the influence of demons through a number of avenues, such as habitual patterns of personal sinfulness. Some authors include the use of alcohol and street drugs as well as the abuse of legitimate medications among venues that may lead to demonization. "Possession of charms and amulets, and objects associated with occult practices, may also make one open to demonic influence. Astrology, Tarot cards, Ouija boards and games like *Dungeons and Dragons* may become conduits of demonic influence."[57]

Some people, as Bufford notes, believe that demonization does not always result from personal sin. A phenomenon known as "ancestral influence" (parental sins) can be at fault. Though not unanimously accepted,[58] some writers maintain that demon possession can be brought about by indirect means. Ed Murphy, one of the most influential writers in the field of demonic warfare, suggests that some Christians are born demonized through a process known by various names: generational sin, familial sin, demonic transference, demonic inheritance, or the law of the inheritance of evil. The most likely means by which such demonization can occur is through active participation in the occult or through child abuse.[59]

---

56 Dawson, *Taking Our Cities for God*, 28.

57 See Roger K. Bufford, *Counseling and the Demonic*, Resources for Christian Counseling, vol. 17 (Dallas, TX: Word Books, 1988), 108.

58 See Dickason, *Angels, Elect and Evil*, 108-110

59 See Murphy, *The Handbook for Spiritual Warfare*, 438 and "We are at War," in *Wrestling with Dark Angels*, 68-69.

The bottom line in all of this is simple: People can be possessed or demonized by evil spirits with or without their consent. Christians and non-Christians alike can be "infected" by demonic beings in the same way we can be infected by the common cold. The peculiar thing about the common cold is the insidious manner in which it is caught. A cold is hardly ever anticipated. We certainly know when we have caught one, but we can seldom tell exactly how we contracted it. It could be the woman who sneezed on the bus the other day. Or perhaps the usher who shook our hand in church. He certainly didn't look too well! Or maybe we caught it in the bathroom. Who knows? It is in the very nature of a cold virus to spread easily and quickly. However, no one contracts the AIDS virus simply by going for a walk, shaking someone's hand or using a public bathroom. Something quite unusual has to happen to develop this illness.

Though demonic warfare authors do not use the common cold analogy, the method by which they believe demons infect human beings is very important to understand. In fact, the unpredictable character of demon infection is one of the core beliefs of demonic warfare and the reason why spiritual warfare specialists are so adamant about warning people about demons. According to the specialists, even if we take all the necessary precautions, such as avoiding occult or New Age practices, it is still possible for us to provide a "foothold" for demonic beings to enter our lives without us being consciously aware of it. Like terrorist attacks, one never knows when, where or how they will occur. Christians who fully integrate this model will live in a state of perpetual siege.

The concept of "footholds" or "entry points" is one of the main reasons why it is said to be so difficult to protect oneself against demonic influence. A foothold is a spiritual weakness by which demons enter into a person.[60] Traumatic events can allegedly leave believers and unbelievers open to demonic oppression. A child who is beaten, abused sexually or witnesses an act of extreme violence is placed in a position of vulnerability. The same is true for a woman who is raped. Not only can a demon gain an entry point in such cases, but the demon also gains a "legal right" to live in the

---

60 See for example, Charles H. Kraft, *Defeating Dark Angels. Breaking Demonic Oppression in The Believer's Life* (Ann Arbor, MI: Servant, 1992), 121-123. See also Murphy, "We are at War," 68, 70.

person. Charles H. Kraft relates this interesting story:

> Jim was hurt badly as a child by many adults. His grandmother and a hired man regularly beat him. The latter abused him sexually as well. Jim's natural and understandable reaction was to be angry at them and others who had mistreated him. When Jim came to me for ministry at about age forty-five, inside him was a seething jumble of hateful emotions that sometimes erupted into incidents when he would lose control and beat his wife. Intense guilt and remorse followed, accompanied by extreme frustration over his lack of self-control. His violence had ruined three previous marriages, and his fourth appeared headed for divorce as well. He was angry at himself, his abusers, and God, and he could find no relief. Though Jim's childhood reactions were normal and, to some extent, necessary for survival, retaining them had weakened his system and given a demon of rage both an entry point and a legal right to live in him.[61]

But it does not end there. Spiritual warfare specialists state that entry points can occur in our ancestral past. In other words, they believe that demons may have gained entry into our ancestral line through means such as acts of extreme violence, involvement in occult movements or witchcraft. In fact, the list of sins providing these entry points covers the whole range of human behavior. On the *Shield of Faith Ministries* website, the host provides an extensive catalog of practices that can generate generational curses.[62] Such demons are subsequently "inherited" by the descendants. Proponents often appeal to such generational sins or curses in order to explain the presence of chronic illnesses such as migraine headaches and back pain, as well as present habitual sins. Although they are careful not to tie every human physical or psychological affliction to such generational curses, many of them will nevertheless thoroughly investigate the possibility. The following quote from a website devoted to demon possession is a typical example:

---

61 Murphy, "We are at War," 122.

62 1. Adultery/pre-marital sex; 2. Abortion; 3. Alcohol/drugs; 4. Anger; 5. Anxiety/worry/fear/terror; 6. Bitterness/control; 7. Covetousness/idolatry; 8. Critical spirit/judgment; 9. Depression/discouragement; 10. Despair/suicidal thoughts; 11. Envy/jealousy; 12. Ingratitude; 13. Isolation; 14. Laziness/lying/deceit; 15. Lust/sexual perversion/pornography/homosexuality; 16. Manipulation; 17. Murder/violence/suicide; 18. Men hating women/misogyny/incest; 19. Occult/occult practices/rebellion/spirit of witchcraft; 20. Rejection; 21. Passivity; 22. Perfectionism; 23. Pride/intolerance/prejudice/pride of life; 24. Self-loathing/ self-hatred; 25. Stealing/greed. For more details, see: Shield of Faith Ministries, "Generational Sins and Weaknesses Checklist," http://www.shieldofaith.org/resources/Library/generational_sins_and_weaknesses. htm (accessed September 25, 2002).

700 years before Maria was born her great-great-grandfather was a Mayan High Priest. In an [*sic*] ceremony to their god Chtualupa all children who would follow from his lineage would be dedicated to the god Chtualupa. From this point onward a Generational Curse would follow his descendants. Demons associated with this curse would "Co-Inhabit" "possess" those born from the Mayan High Priest's lineage. Because of this Generational Curse, Maria would have extreme difficulty in understanding and hearing the gospel. If she did understand and receive it she would have a very cold walk with Jesus Christ. The demons indwelling in her would prevent her from experiencing His joy.[63]

The devastating impact of spirits acquired in this manner is explained by the fact that certain types of demons, such as occult and inherited demons, are said to be stronger in general than demons picked up in other ways.[64] For example, the earliest ancestor in my family to reach the New World was a corsair: He was, in fact, the captain of a pirate ship. According to demonic warfare model, the acts of violence he undoubtedly committed would have created demonic entry points that would have affected my family line into the present. Fred C. Dickason estimates that ancestral involvement is the "chief cause of demonization." He adds, "Well over 95 percent of more than 400 persons I have contacted in my counseling ministry have been demonized because of their ancestors' involvement in occult and demonic activities." [65]

A New Priesthood

the demonic warfare community has its cast of specialists who have the unique knowledge needed to deal with demons. These specialists are said to have a distinctive status, for we are presumably living in the end times and are therefore on the brink of an all-out war with the powers of darkness. As the prospect of war becomes an increasingly imminent and unavoidable reality, it follows that these specialists will be called to take on increasingly central roles. Although these demonic warfare generals liberally share their knowledge, the average Christian is counseled to be extremely cautious in any personal

---

63 "Family Inheritance: Generational Curses," http://www.demonpossession.com/inheritance.html (accessed September 25, 2002).

64 Murphy, "We are at War," 125.

65 Dickason, *Demon Possession*, 221

attempts to deal with demons.

It is assumed that only those with the required spiritual qualifications should deal with higher-level demons. As Wagner points out, not all Christians can deal with just any kind of demon. Some Christians are called to wrestle against "ground-level spirits." Others will combat the "middle-level spirits," that tend to operate through the agency of witches, occultists, New Age channellers and mediums. Finally, only certain Christians will be called to strike against higher level "territorial spirits," that are described as powerful demons who control entire nations, cities or subcultures.[66] The higher ranking the demon, the more necessary it becomes to appeal to the demonic warfare specialist's knowledge and experience. Since average Christians can never know whether they have reached a sufficient level of spirituality, and since it is virtually impossible to determine the type of demon one is dealing with, we are left with little choice but to defer to the specialist. This is especially true when we consider the dire consequences of dealing incompetently with demons: such as the danger of becoming demonized, ill or even being killed.

In that scenario, the demonic warfare specialist plays the role of the priest, prophet or diviner in primitive societies who alone has the special knowledge to manipulate the powers and protect the common people from evil.

How Do They Know?

As most people will recognize, to state something is one thing, but to actually prove it is quite another. So how do these demonic warfare specialists actually know that what they say is in fact a fair and accurate representation of spiritual reality? I am not, of course, the first person to ask the question. In fact, in his book *Confronting the Powers*, Wagner attempts to respond to the criticisms that have come his way because of his unorthodox evangelism approach. [67]

Demonic warfare specialists such as Wagner appeal to three kinds of sources for what they believe: 1) Scripture; 2) words of knowledge; 3) reports of experiences with the demonic world.[68]

The proponents of demonic warfare commonly seek to validate their teachings by appealing to Scripture. In that respect, Ed Murphy's writings

---

66   Wagner, "Spiritual Warfare," 20 and Dawson, *Taking Our Cities for God*, 132.

67   See C. Peter Wagner, *Confronting the Powers. How the New Testament Church Experienced the Power of Strategic-Level Spiritual Warfare* (Ventura, CA: Regal Books, 1996).

68   Wagner, "Spiritual Warfare," 16.

reflect a sincere concern for scriptural accuracy. In fact, unlike many who limit themselves to the New Testament, Murphy goes to great lengths to include a wide range of Old and New Testament passages to document his positions.

Although the majority of these authors deserve some credit for attempting to ground their beliefs and practices in Scripture, a few things must be noted. In most cases, these writers refer to the same few basic texts such as 1 Peter 5:8-9 (*"Your enemy the devil prowls…"*), Luke 11:21-23 (the "strong man" passage), Daniel 10:13 (territorial spirits), or Ephesians 6:12 (*"Our struggle is not against flesh and blood…"*). Where an author endeavors to use a broader scriptural base, I have found that the Bible quickly becomes an indiscriminate source of proof texts used to support whatever position is being presented.

Generally, these additional texts tend to be used without careful consideration for their literary character. Matters such as genre analysis (form criticism), intent (redaction criticism), issues relating to context, both remote and immediate, are given almost no consideration. The only clear hermeneutical criterion that seems to apply is whether the selected texts can be linked to the issue of warfare in one fashion or another. The bottom line here is that little consideration is given to the Bible as a literary work. Rather, the Bible is simply perceived as a way to confirm whatever beliefs and practices the authors advocate. Consequently, they tend to adopt a highly intuitive approach to biblical interpretation. They often short circuit the process of applying sound interpretation principles to the various texts they draw on in developing their ideas; a sort of "cut and paste" method where the Bible mostly confirms a pre-existing framework. As I will demonstrate in the following chapters, there is little scriptural support to warrant the very sophisticated and elaborate model these demonic warfare authors advance. [69]

While the majority of writers contend that their conclusions derive from Scripture, they also readily admit it is not always possible to verify every claim they make from a strictly scriptural perspective. This is particularly true when a specific instance of spiritual deliverance depends on explicit knowledge about the heavenly realm (the "heavenlies"). As Wagner points out, such is particularly the case with the practice of "loosing and binding" (Matt. 16:19).[70] Wagner notes that Christians have the authority to "loose" and "bind," i.e.,

---

69   The reader is invited to compare the interpretations of such commonly-used passages as Daniel 10 and Ephesians 6 with the rigorous interpretation of these passages offered by Page in *Powers of Evil*.

70   Wagner, "Spiritual Warfare," 14-17.

to "loose" people from the power of demons and, in counterpart, to "bind" demons. Wagner, however, is careful to note that Christians cannot do this indiscriminately. For it to be effective, that which is "loosed" or "bound" on earth must already have been "loosed" or "bound" in heaven. Since we have no direct way of knowing what God is doing in heaven, Wagner appeals to what some Pentecostal theologians have called the *rhema* word. Whereas the *logos* word is God's Word found in the canon of Scripture, the *rhema* word is a word from God regarding a specific problem. One example would be the information needed to carry out an exorcism. Such *rhema* words are generally received through the agency of Christians who have a prophetic gift or the gift of spiritual discernment.[71]

[Alert]:
We need to be cautious about conferring credibility on the whole notion of rhema *words. First, even demonic warfare specialists themselves only occasionally use these* rhema *words to confirm their theories. Second, without denying the reality of such occurrences, it is important to underline the highly subjective character of these revelations. They always apply to individual cases, making them limited in scope. Third, these* rhema *words should not be used to prove or disprove major doctrines. God's written word is our primary source of authority for discerning the real nature of the universe, not the subjective impressions of those who may or may not be receiving special messages from God. Demonic warfare is a critical issue: the conclusions we draw will affect our lives and the lives of those we minister to in ways we can barely imagine. We must base those conclusions on the best evidence available and only that.*

The main source of information regarding demonic warfare is found in the multitude of stories and anecdotes reflecting personal spiritual warfare experiences. These stories originate from all over the world and are broadly used to illustrate and validate the demonic warfare writers' claims. There are literally thousands of stories that are available to validate a particular understanding of the relationship between the human and demonic spheres. But perhaps even more dangerously, these stories become a virtual grid of interpretation through which the Bible is read. Too often, it is not experience that is filtered through a biblical grid, but the Bible that is filtered through experience.

---

71 Wagner, "Spiritual Warfare," 15-16.

In and of itself, there is nothing wrong with using experiences to demonstrate the validity of a belief, an idea or a hypothesis. In fact, our whole scientific method is based on the empirical principle. We are constantly in the process of testing whether our perception of reality is accurate or not. We also often appeal to personal experience to give witness to the reality of Christ in our lives. We must, however, be keenly aware of the limitations inherent in using anecdotes and personal stories to describe ultimate reality.

First, the significance of any personal experience is rarely ever self-evident, particularly when it comes to testing and claiming truth in the spiritual realm. The interpretation we give to any personal experience or anecdote depends primarily on the worldview we begin with. For example, a primitive tribe member who falls ill will likely attribute his illness to evil spirits, a curse or some enchantment. The tribe member will seek out a sorcerer or a shaman to find a way to thwart the spirit's action. The ultimate cause of such illness will be traced back to some sin or to an enemy's action. A North American will experience the same sickness and believe it came from exposure to bacteria, a virus or an identifiable physiological cause. It would not normally occur to such a person to look for a spiritual cause to the illness. Two people experiencing the same symptoms with two widely divergent interpretations, all because of differing assumptions about the nature of reality.

Second, we often overlook the complexity of human perception. In fact, how we perceive reality is the end product of a tremendously complex biochemical process where 100 billion neurons constantly create what amounts to a "virtual" universe right inside our skulls. Normally, the steady stream of data used to reconstruct our environment represents a reasonably accurate reflection of reality. Under certain circumstances, however, this is not the case. For a variety of reasons—such as extreme stress, trauma, chemical imbalances or even a disease like Alzheimer's—the brain can begin to misfire resulting in various kinds of misperceptions. Even without the presence of a physiological dysfunction, interpretation of reality—whether it relates to a historical event or determining responsibility in a traffic accident—is far from being foolproof. Because subjectivity is inherent to human perception, we use various avenues to help us discriminate between a reasonably accurate perception of reality and a faulty one. For example, dramatic reports of alien encounters are simply not sufficient to prove an alien presence on the earth.

In this respect, one of the major problems with many spiritual warfare specialists is their indiscriminate use of anecdotal reports coupled with an alarming absence of intellectual or academic rigor. For example, Wagner often uses anecdotal material to support a particular scriptural interpretation. The illustrations tend to be second-hand stories that make gratuitous or incidental connections to support various claims. Here is an example:

> Underestimating the power of the enemy is a major danger, and some have paid the price for falling into it. I know of several American pastors who have taken on territorial spirits and ended up leaving the ministry because of immorality. A Japanese pastor told me of a church member who brought a family idol to be destroyed, but also said he had been warned that if it was destroyed someone in his family would die. He burned the idol in the patio of the church, and within six months a cousin's son died and his wife lost her first child. A Presbyterian pastor in Gahana ordered a tree which had become a satanic shrine to be cut down. When the last branch was lopped off, the pastor dropped dead.[72]

Some readers might support the cause-and-effect connections between the desecrations and the following tragic events. But I contend that they are only coherent and plausible within the narrow confines of Wagner's own worldview. It is not surprising that such inferences may have some degree of plausibility since worldviews are by definition self-coherent. But there is no necessary link between a worldview's self-coherence and whether or not it accurately reflects ultimate reality. In this case, there are simply no objective criteria to demonstrate the validity of Wagner's conclusions. The connection between the tree/shrine and the death of the pastor may be puzzling—even intriguing—but it does not constitute an objective proof of a cause-and-effect link between the two.

I also contend that the kind of logical leap needed to establish a strict relationship of cause-and-effect between events that chronologically follow

---

72 Wagner, *"Spiritual Warfare,"* 19.

each other is much more consistent with magical thinking than with anything else. In fact, I find Wagner's methodology very disconcerting. Such an approach to determining truth implies that any negative experience—from a flat tire to a loved one's accidental death—would need to be interpreted in the context of a conceptual universe where the real causes of these events could not be identified through normal investigative methods. At best, this makes it impossible to ever truly determine the real causes behind various events. At worst, it leads people to identify false causes. It is no wonder that many of those who embrace this worldview experience fears, uncertainties and doubts of all kinds. In such a world, we can never know for certain whether a man's death was the result of an icy patch on the highway or of a careless and even unknown exposure to a demonic object. We may ask ourselves this question: Do we live in a world dominated by evil and occult forces that forever threaten to overwhelm us at the least sign of weakness or spiritual carelessness? If the answer is yes, then we must take every possible precaution to immunize ourselves against the occult powers that constantly hover over us. We must ensure we have access to demonic warfare specialists to protect ourselves and our children against spiritual terrorism.

Such a view of the universe may excite our imagination. It may even agree with what some churches teach or what popular culture projects about the demonic. But the more worthwhile question is this: Does this worldview reflect reality? We must find out the answer, for the Christian faith is not about living in fantasy; the primary task of the Christian is to deal with reality.

Chapter 2:

Towards a Biblical Worldview

Introduction

Much of what is written about demonic warfare is impossible to substantiate. Can someone become possessed through some kind of demonic infection? Do evil spirits really belong to a satanic organization where each is assigned a rank and a particular role? Can demons really infiltrate objects or remain attached to places? Although demonic warfare specialists can speak extensively and authoritatively about demons, the reality is that there is little explicit evidence—biblical or otherwise—to support their views. Does that mean we are condemned to live in complete uncertainty? Not at all!

First, we need to avoid seeing these claims in isolation. The teachings are part of a wider system that constitutes a distinct and coherent worldview. In some sense, this is where we face our major difficulty. As a whole, the ideology is plausible. Once we accept the assumptions popularly held about demonic warfare, then the various aspects of the overall belief system make sense. If, for example, I believe that demons constantly plot to make us question their existence, then I will immediately be suspicious of anyone who suggests that demons may not exist or may not operate according to the model I am familiar with. I will perceive that person as a tool the devil is using to mislead me rather than as a valid conversation partner. Though that perception may be absolutely false, it remains credible because it agrees with a given set of assumptions that I believe to be true. It is effectively impossible to challenge the way certain events are interpreted from within the same worldview "bubble" that provides the underlying beliefs.

Instead of simply trying to evaluate some of the more common demonic warfare beliefs and practices, this chapter will focus more specifically on the worldview underlying it. This approach intends to develop a tool that will help us ascertain whether and to what extent the worldview reflects and corresponds to what Scripture teaches about our world.

Some readers will no doubt immediately balk at the notion of a coherent biblical worldview. Is it not possible to make the Bible say anything we want? Can we not concoct any worldview we wish by carefully selecting passages that support our preconceptions? The objection is partly valid and must be taken seriously. We need some kind of control factor. We have to have a common standard that we can use to arrive at a picture of the biblical worldview. Fortunately, such a standard is available: the Genesis Creation account (Genesis 1-3).

Rationale

The Creation narrative in Genesis 1-3 represents an ideal starting point because it contains the theological foundation of the entire Bible. These three chapters represent the basic theological DNA of biblical revelation and must therefore be given precedence in developing a biblical worldview. The reason behind what will be for many an audacious and surprising statement is linked first and foremost to the kind of literature Genesis 1-3 embodies. The Creation account, by virtue of the literary genre it represents, was designed to provide the blueprint of a new worldview. Its primary function was to propose an alternative to the Canaanite/Mesopotamian[1] worldview the Israelites had absorbed in 400 years of Egyptian captivity. While the notion of constructing something as ambitious as a worldview from such a narrow range of texts will no doubt come as a surprise to some readers, I would, however, argue for the legitimacy of the approach by appealing to the special nature and function of the Creation story.

The Purpose of the Creation Story

In order to more fully appreciate the presence of the Creation account in the book of Genesis, it will be helpful to better understand the role creation stories played in the ancient world. Creation stories are not unique to Hebrew literature. Archeologists have uncovered several examples in ancient Egypt, Mesopotamia and throughout the world. These accounts are generally referred to as myths. In popular culture, the word "myth" generally denotes something that is false or not based on fact. When someone says: "That's a myth," the person usually means that the story is bunk. However, scholars refer to mythology to describe ancient accounts that provide a comprehensive and coherent view of: the world, the nature of the divine and the origin, role and destiny of humankind. These myths are extremely valuable, for they provide an insight into the very heart of a culture's worldview.

---

1   In this book, I use "Canaanite" and "Mesopotamian" somewhat interchangeably, since Mesopotamian culture was widely diffused in the West. See Gordon J. Wenham, *Genesis 1-15*, Word Biblical Commentary (Waco, TX: Word Books, 1987), xliv

While Genesis 1-3 plays a role similar to that of other creation accounts found in the ancient Near East, it is set in a unique context. According to Exodus 5:22 through 6:8,[2] God gave Moses a twofold mandate. First, Moses was to deliver the Hebrew people from their Egyptian oppressors. Second, he was to communicate to his people an accurate picture of Yahweh so they might adopt him as their God. The first part of that mandate was relatively simple. The second part was considerably more complex, for it involved transforming the Hebrews' worldview and changing their loyalty. This was necessary because after 400 years in Egypt, the Hebrew people had forgotten about the God of Abraham, Isaac and Jacob and had essentially embraced a pagan vision of the world that can only be characterized as Mesopotamian. We tend not to think of the Hebrews in Egypt as pagans, but it is important to point out in order to fully comprehend the function and the importance of the biblical Creation account.

Out of Egypt

Exodus 16:2-3 tells us that soon after the Israelites had fled from Egypt, they complained bitterly about their new living arrangements.

The whole congregation of the Israelites complained against Moses and Aaron in the wilderness. The Israelites said to them, "If only we had died by the hand of the LORD in the land of Egypt, when we sat by the fleshpots and ate our fill of bread; for you have brought us out into this wilderness to kill this whole assembly with hunger."

A similar wish is uttered in chapter 17.

From the wilderness of Sin the whole congregation of the Israelites journeyed by stages, as the LORD commanded. They camped at Rephidim, but there was no water for the people to drink. The people quarreled with Moses, and said, "Give us water to drink." Moses said to them, "Why do you quarrel with me? Why do you test the LORD?"
But the people thirsted there for water; and the people complained against Moses and said, "Why did you bring us out of Egypt, to kill us and our children and livestock with thirst?" (Exod. 17:1-3).

---

2   On the significance of this text for biblical theology, see Elmer Martens, *God's Design: A Focus on Old Testament Theology*, 3d ed. (N. Richland Hills, TX: Bibal, 1998 [1981]), 3-19.

At this point in their journey, not only did the people wish they had never left Egypt, but they became convinced that Yahweh wanted them dead. What can explain such a reversal on the part of a people who had just been liberated from a cruel oppressor? I find it difficult to believe that hunger was their only motivation; there was more going on.

The Hebrews' longing for their pre-liberation days can be linked to certain beliefs they held about Yahweh's true character. The real issue was the perception they had of God. These texts indicate that they did not trust this new God. The moment they encountered a major challenge, they reverted back to a default theological position that is a hallmark of the Canaanite/Mesopotamian worldview: The gods are ultimately evil and untrustworthy.

Numbers 16 and 17 reveal that the Hebrews were no different from their neighbors regarding their fundamental beliefs about the divine. That the Hebrews were suspicious of this new God is particularly puzzling in view of the extraordinary miracles they had recently witnessed: the 10 plagues, the crossing of the Red Sea and the destruction of Pharaoh's army. The perception that the gods were evil eventually overshadowed their initial conclusions about Yahweh's miraculous acts of deliverance. It had all been too good to be true. They had grossly misinterpreted this new God's intentions. Far from desiring their liberation, he only saved them from the Egyptians so he could more easily exterminate them in the desert. How exquisitely cruel! It was all a pretense. To put it crudely, they believed they were the butt of a divine practical joke.

When the Hebrews ended up in the desert with nothing to eat, their suspicions were confirmed: This new God was no different from any other god. He was only more devious and subtle, like an Alfred Hitchcock of the gods! Amazingly enough, Yahweh responded to this open rebellion by providing physical sustenance (Exod. 16:8; 17:5-6). The people were given one more opportunity to arrive at more appropriate conclusions.

The Golden Calf

Exodus 32:1-6 reports another incident that underlines the Hebrew worldview's pagan character. When Moses went up to Mount Sinai, the people immediately clamored for Aaron to make a golden calf for them to worship. If this wasn't bad enough, we learn that after they ate and drank, they got up to "play"—a Hebrew euphemism that denotes sexual activity. The problem was not simply one of morality. The Israelites were engaged in activities that were appropriate in the context of a fertility cult. Canaanites believed that Baal, often portrayed as a bull, generated fertility through sexual intercourse with his consort, the goddess Anat (or Asherah). Canaanite religion closely linked human sexuality with worship.[3] Canaanites believed that the ritual re-enactment of Baal and Anat's physical union would foster fertility in the land.

These two examples show the extent to which the Hebrew worldview had become corrupted over the 400 years of Egyptian captivity. If Moses intended to create a nation to reflect the character of this new God, he would have to establish a worldview that would effectively compete with the Hebrews' false beliefs about the divine, the universe and humanity.

In the ancient world, creation narratives served as vehicles of communication to transmit a worldview. This is the agenda that drives the development of Genesis 1-3.[4] Much more than a story designed to entertain children around the campfire, the Genesis Creation account was

---

3   Israelite law strongly forbids such an instrumental view of human sexuality (Lev. 19:29 and Deut. 23:18-19).

4   Many biblical scholars do not agree with a dating of this text that locates it in the Mosaic period. Most critical scholars, in fact, attribute a final redactional date for Genesis 1-3 sometime in the post-exilic era. Be that as it may, it is important to note that there is in fact little evidence to suggest any date for this text, let alone such a late one. Up until a few decades ago, critical scholars held to the literary theory known as JEDP. According to this theory, the Pentateuch can be divided into sections indicating various sources originating from different eras and regions. Although no new hypothesis has received the general assent of the scholarly community, the JEDP theory no longer receives unanimous endorsement. Following Wenham (Genesis 1-15, xlii-xlv), I think there is sufficient ground to support the existence of a creation story that would have encompassed the most important ideas now attested in the canonical narrative. The existence of such a story would be absolutely compatible with Moses's mandate to create a distinct political entity. For a more detailed assessment of the documentary theory, see U. Cassuto, *The Documentary Hypothesis and the Composition of the Pentateuch: Eight Lectures*, tr. by I. Abrahams (Jerusalem: Magnes, 1961); R. Alter, *The Art of Biblical Narrative* (New York, NY: Basic Books, 1981); D. Garrett, *Rethinking Genesis: The Sources and Authorship of the First Book of the Pentateuch* (Grand Rapids, MI: Baker, 1991); G. Maier, "How did Moses Compose the Pentateuch?" *Stulos Theological Journal*, vol. 1 (1993):157-161; A. F. Campbell and M. A. O'Brien, *Sources of the Pentateuch: Texts, Introductions, Annotations* (Minneapolis, MN: Fortress, 1993), 10-15.

first and foremost a polemic text![5] It was written to teach the Hebrews about the true nature of reality and to provide a dynamic alternative to the Canaanite/Mesopotamian worldview the Israelites had assimilated during their time in Egypt. I cannot overemphasize the significance of this point. If the Creation story was indeed designed to address worldview issues and to serve as an alternative, then this text must occupy a central place in any attempt to develop a biblical worldview.

What exactly was the Creation story competing against? Exodus 16, 17 and 32 indicate that the Hebrews in Egypt had, over time, adopted a belief system that was very similar to what was commonly found in Canaan and Mesopotamia. But what exactly did Canaanites or Mesopotamians believe at that time? The most effective way to answer that question is to examine ancient Near Eastern myths.

The Canaanite/Mesopotamian Worldview
Ancient Near Eastern Myths
The most widely known creation myths of the ancient Near East are the *Atrahasis* and the *Enuma Elish*.[6]

The *Myth of Atrahasis*[7] begins by describing the desperate plight of the lower gods, the *Igigi*, who are condemned to endlessly performing heavy work in the service of the higher gods, the *Anunnaki*. At some point, the *Igigi* decide to go on strike, destroy their tools and surround

---

5 For more details on the polemic character of the Creation story, see Yehezkel Kaufmann, *The Religion of Israel: From Its Beginnings to the Babylonian Exile* (Chicago, IL: University of Chicago Press, 1960), 60-63; Jean Bottéro, "Le Dieu de la bible," in *La plus belle histoire de Dieu: Qui est le Dieu de la bible?* (Paris: Seuil, 1997); *Naissance de Dieu: la Bible et l'historien* (Paris: Gallimard, 1986). See also Gerhard F. Hasel, "The Polemic Nature of the Genesis Cosmology," *The Evangelical Quarterly* 46 (1974):81-102.

6 A translation of these myths is found in James B. Pritchard, *Ancient Near Eastern Texts Relating to the Old Testament*, 3rd ed. (Princeton, NJ: Princeton University Press, 1969). See also Victor H. Matthews and Don C. Benjamin, *Old Testament Parallels*, 2nd ed. (New York/Mahwah, NJ: Paulist Press, 1997 [1991], 9-18 (Enuma Elish), 31-40 (Atrahasis) and Stephanie Dalley, *Myths from Mesopotamia* (Oxford: Oxford University Press, 1989), 228-277 (Enuma Elish) and 1-38 (Atrahasis).

7 The Myth of Atrahasis is the most ancient mythological writing we have at our disposal. The great poem is written in Akkadian and dated prior to the oldest fragments recovered from King Ammisaduqa's reign (1646-1626 B.C.), fourth successor of Hammurabi of Babylon. The title is derived from the name of the hero that plays the role of the king of the country, *Atrahasis*, which means "the exceptional wise" (see Jean Bottéro, *La plus vieille religion en Mésopotamie*. Folio/histoire [Paris: Gamillard, 1998], 199).

the divine palace. The *Anunnaki*, fearing starvation, agree to create a new mortal and short-lived creature–man–to take over the *Igigi*'s work. The plan works wonders. The lower-class gods are freed from their drudgery, and life for the *Anunnaki* resumes its normal course. But a complication arises: What the humans lack in lifespan, they make up for in their ability to reproduce. Over time, the humans become so numerous and noisy that the god Enlil has trouble sleeping. The problem is so serious that he seeks to utterly destroy humankind by alternatively ordering a plague, a famine and a universal flood. Each time, humanity is saved, *in extremis*, by the intervention of the god Enki.

In the Babylonian myth known as the Enuma Elish,[8] we learn that the earth was created following a great battle between the Babylonian god Marduk and the goddess Tiamat. At the end of the battle, Marduk, who had defeated and killed the monster Tiamat, used her skin to form the heavens and the rest of her body to create the earth. Then, Marduk requested the execution and body of the god, Kingu. With Kingu's blood, Marduk created the *lullu*—Man—so that the lower gods, the *Igigi*, would no longer have to work.

The Mesopotamian Worldview: A Brief Overview

These two myths represent an excellent starting point in understanding what the ancients believed about the gods and the origin of the world; and more particularly, what they believed about the origin and role of humanity. The following points represent a brief synopsis of the ancient Canaanite and Mesopotamian worldview: [9]

- The world was created in the context of violence, conflict and war.
- The divine world was composed of a multitude of deities who expressed their presence and influence through the physical world. (This is what I will refer later to as the mythologization of the universe.)

---

8   The Enuma Elish was compiled around 1100 B.C. from various Sumerian and Amorite traditions. For a more detailed summary of the myth, see Thorkild Jacobsen, "Mesopotamian religion." *Encyclopædia Britannica Online*, http://www.britannica.com/eb/article-68282 (accessed September 27, 2007).

9   For more details, I recommend Jean Bottéro, *Religion in Ancient Mesopotamia*, tr. by Teresa Lavender Fagan (Chicago, IL: The University of Chicago Press, 2001).

- The gods were evil, unreliable, violent, unpredictable, inconsistent and untrustworthy.
- The deities were part of a hierarchical organization.
- Human beings were slaves whose only use was to serve the gods.
- Human beings had no friends in the universe. They ultimately had no one to whom they could appeal.
- Human beings had no hope for a better future. Their function was strictly utilitarian. At best, they could hope to live a life without being unduly noticed by the gods.
- Human life was characterized by uncertainty and fear. People lived in a universe where disaster and affliction could strike at any time.
- People lived in doubt and ignorance of the will of the gods. They constantly sought to appease the gods. If calamity struck a man, it was assumed that a god had been offended or that a demon had been summoned against him. The implications were staggering: Not only was this man ignorant of which god he had offended, but he also had no idea of the exact nature of the offense. With a notion of justice that did not necessarily correspond to the more fluid and ever-shifting justice of the gods, such a man lived in a world devoid of universal moral rules.
- Human beings had no intrinsic sense of identity and self worth. They were born slaves and would die as such.
- Human beings were the powerless victims of divine cosmic forces. Overwhelming powers determined their past, their present and would inexorably shape their future.
- People depended on "spiritual" specialists (diviners, prophets, astrologers, etc.) to discover the ever-elusive will of the gods and to protect them against their wrath.

This, in a nutshell, is what Israel's neighbors believed. And this is the belief system the Hebrews themselves came to assimilate during their stay in Egypt. The Genesis Creation account was designed to provide a radically different and revolutionary alternative to that worldview.

A Striking Similarity

In the comparative table below, I have set some basic elements of the Canaanite/Mesopotamian worldview side by side with the demonic warfare model. In many respects, the similarities between the two are striking [10] and the implications of these similarities should not be lost on the reader. If the Genesis Creation account was developed to provide an alternative to the ancient Canaanite/Mesopotamian worldview and if the demonic warfare model proposes a worldview similar to that of the ancient Mesopotamians, then it follows that the creation account will also represent a penetrating critique of the demonic warfare model.

A Comparative Outline of Two Worldviews

Ancient Mesopotamian	Demonic Warfare
Creation originates in violence.	Humanity's creation is set against a backdrop of conflict and war.
Mythologization of the universe.	Mythologization of the universe.
The malevolent influence of the gods is mediated through the environment.	The malevolent influence of demons is mediated through the environment.
The gods operate within a highly organized hierarchy.	Demons operate within a highly organized hierarchy.
Human experience is characterized by conflict with the gods.	The Christian experience is characterized by conflict with demonic powers.
Human experience is characterized by fear and uncertainty.	The Christian experience is characterized by fear and uncertainty.
The Mesopotamian's fate is contingent on the gods.	The Christian is constantly living under the possible influence of the demonic world.
Mesopotamians are dependent on diviners to exorcize their world.	Christians are dependent on spiritual warfare "specialists" to exorcize their world.

---

10   The reader should note that Gregory Boyd finds support for a warfare worldview in the Bible in the numerous mythologies of various ancient and contemporary peoples throughout the world. He writes, "Their mythologies reveal the nearly universal conviction that the battlefield appearance of the world is the result of a real battle that once took place, or is still taking place, in 'nonordinary' reality" (*God at War*, 15).

Genesis 1-3: The Blueprint of A Biblical Worldview
A Revolutionary Vision of the World

By all accounts, the biblical Creation story remains the most remarkable text ever to emerge from the ancient world. The powerful concepts challenged everything ancient Mesopotamians held as absolute truth. Though the Creation story is not unique in the type of literature it represents, it is, however, in a category of its own: The worldview it embodies is unlike anything else in the ancient world. [11]

The Creation narrative has often been misunderstood or severely curtailed in its use in the church and in society. For instance, it was most aggressively recruited in the late 19th century to challenge Darwinism and it has been used ever since in the evolutionist/creationist debate. Regardless of the merits of that conversation, the Creation story was not primarily designed to combat evolutionism or to determine whether God created the universe in six 24-hour days or in six long periods of history. Though these are critical questions, they remain our questions and not necessarily those the text was written to answer. Without discounting the use of Genesis 1-3 in such debates, it is crucial to determine the primary issues the Creation story was originally designed to address.

By virtue of its literary genre, the Creation account's most basic function is to address a broad range of worldview issues. The Creation story of Genesis 1-3 outlines a worldview that ably competed against the prevailing Canaanite/Mesopotamian beliefs. It teaches about the ultimate nature of reality. It is what I have called a foundational text as it establishes fundamental truths about God, humanity and nature. Moreover—and in this lies the true significance of this text—not only is it foundational, it is also profoundly subversive of some aspects of human culture. Its teachings act like an acid on the structures of dehumanization and exploitation that societies tend to create and reproduce in every generation. The following pages examine some of the most critical elements of the Creation story.

---

11   See in particular Hasel, "The Polemic Nature of the Genesis Cosmology," 81-102. Yehezkel Kaufmann more broadly examines the unique character of the Israelite religion in his book *The Religion of Israel* (Chicago, IL: The University of Chicago Press, 1960).

The Demythologization of the Universe

There is something remarkable in that most people in the Western world do not worship the sun, the moon or the stars. In fact, most of us find the notion of worshiping the sun quite ludicrous. And yet the question remains: Why do we not worship the heavenly bodies, the earth or the life force in the trees like millions of people have done since the dawn of time? I doubt it is because we are exceptionally smart, prodigiously enlightened or even superior. I am convinced that the only way to explain why we do not worship nature or sacrifice children to Baal, Molech or any other divinity, is because of the subversive work of the Bible in our culture. In fact, had the biblical text been completely absent from Western culture, I am absolutely convinced that we would still be nature worshipers today.

The first sentence of the Creation account provides the cornerstone of the biblical worldview: "*In the beginning God created the heavens and the earth*" (Gen. 1:1 NIV).

Only One God

This text states that there is only one God, and that this God created the world. The "heavens and the earth" encompasses the entire known universe. By the standards of its time, this is a most remarkable and surprising declaration. This simple statement contains the seeds of the eventual demise and destruction of the entire Mesopotamian mythical universe. In one swipe, this text fatally undermines the world of the gods and their powers. It truly was the toll that marked the end of the age of the gods and the beginning of the age of men. Genesis 1:1 affirms the absolute sovereignty of God over creation and distinguishes the person of God from the created order. At this juncture of history, it was a vision that departed radically from everything humans believed about the gods.

Throughout history, humans have consistently believed that the divine is intrinsically entwined with the physical world, a view we generally call pantheism. C. S. Lewis, in *Mere Christianity*, points out that in pantheism, the divine and the physical universe are believed to be almost one and the same. The divine is beyond good and evil. It is indistinguishable from the universe; so that if one could conceive of the universe disappearing, God or the gods would also be extinguished. The first verse of Genesis 1 is diametrically opposed to such a perception of the divine. The text conjures up the picture of a God who imagines and makes the universe in the same way an artist creates a work of art. To borrow from Lewis: "A painter is not a picture, and he does not die if his picture is destroyed."[12]

The author does not attempt to communicate to the Hebrews that Elohim is one god amongst many. Genesis 1 could not be any clearer: Elohim is the only God and sole creator of the universe. The notion of an only God, who is completely distinct from the physical realm did not naturally emerge in Israel. The idea was as foreign for the Hebrews as it was for their neighbors, perhaps explaining why Israel repeatedly turned to foreign gods or sought to transform Yahweh into a mutation of Baal. Though the people of Israel struggled with idolatry—as the prophetic literature points out all too clearly—Genesis 1 leaves no doubt as to what the great theologian was trying to convey. Elohim is the only God from whom everything proceeds. End of the story!

The End of Magic

"In the beginning, God created..." can best be compared to a cosmic vacuum cleaner. A thundering declaration that freed the universe of the multitude of gods and demons that populated the ancient world.

For ancient Mesopotamians who lived under the constant threat of hostile deities—who sought to immunize themselves against these powers and gain some control over their destiny through magical formulas and rituals—the Creation account's opening sentence offered a world of new possibilities. By draining the physical universe of its divine essence, this text accomplished two things. First, it annihilated the conceptual framework that made it possible to believe in magic. In the ancient world, magical formulas had no power in and of themselves. Magic only became powerful if the gods were willing to act upon human wishes expressed through magical acts: wishes for fertility, protection from one's enemies, etc.

Although scholars have long held that ancient people believed that curses, blessings and magical rituals were contingent on the inherent

---

12   C. S. Lewis, *Mere Christianity* (New York, NY: HarperSanFrancisco, 2001[1952], 40.

power of the word,[13] there is simply no evidence to that effect. Ancient Near Eastern documents consistently link the effectiveness of magical incantations, curses and blessings to the intervention of the gods, not to a mysterious power of the word.

The notion that magical powers could mysteriously influence human life was one of the beliefs the author of the creation account was attempting to counteract. The text could not have been more explicit. By emptying the physical universe of its deities, the author destroyed the very existence of magical power and the possibility of manipulating it. It was a way of declaring: "A piece of wood is just a piece of wood!"[14] No gods... no magic!

In the very process of eliminating the foundation for magic—by erasing the very existence of the gods on whom the powers of magic depended— this text had a surprising side effect: It set into motion the conditions that would eventually make it possible to develop empirical science.

Without the appearance of an authoritative text to challenge and undermine nature's divine character, it is virtually impossible to conceive of a rigorous and fully developed scientific model. As surprising as this may sound, the reason behind this observation is remarkably simple: We cannot investigate, analyze or dissect what we worship and fear! The Creation account essentially initiated a process of demythologization that characterized the physical universe in terms of "object" rather than "subject." It set the stage for humanity to take its rightful place in the universe: Not as terrorized slaves of divine cosmic powers, but as the world's rulers or superintendents.

In the Mesopotamian worldview, the universe was the seat of divine consciousness and humanity was its object. The divine beings expressed

---

13 This thesis, at least as it pertains to Israel and its environment, was first proposed by J. Pedersen (*Israel. Its Life and Culture*, vol. 1 [London: Oxford University Press, 1926 [1920]]) and has been the object of near-consensus by the scholarly community. As attractive as that thesis might be, there is simply not a shred of evidence to support it. In a comprehensive study of the curse in the Ancient Near East, I have demonstrated that the effectiveness of the curse is always contingent on the intervention of the gods (see *Le motif imprécatoire chez les prophètes bibliques du 8è siècle A.C. à la lumière du Proche-orient ancien*, unpublished doctoral dissertation [Université de Montréal, 1993], 25-133). T. G. Crawford independently reached the same conclusion in regards to the Syro-Palestinian region in the Iron Age (see *Blessing and Curse in Syro-Palestinian Inscriptions of the Iron Age*, AUS, series 7, TR, vol. 120 (New York, NY: Peter Lang, 1992).

14 This is the essence of the prophet Isaiah's sarcastic observations about idols in Isaiah 44:13-19.

their presence in the elements of the physical universe; humanity was the object of their actions. In the Creation account, the roles are dramatically reversed. The physical universe is stripped of its divine consciousness allowing humans to take their proper place as self-determining agents. The world is no longer populated by evil powers bent on disrupting human life, and physical objects no longer express divine essence. The universe is no longer an object of worship or fear. Not only are the gods erased right out of existence, but by the repeated allusion to Creation's "goodness," the great theologian proclaims to all men and women that they live in a friendly universe!

Without an authoritative declaration to challenge nature's deification and humanity's objectification, it is impossible to imagine, let alone propose, an alternative. The ancient Egyptians and Greeks had, from time to time, great insights into the nature of reality, but these insights never led to the complete abandonment of idolatry and the development of a fully integrated scientific model. [15]

As a case in point, the Greek philosopher Aristarchus (ca. 310-230 B.C.) had, long before Copernicus, voiced the theory that the earth revolved around the sun. Aristarchus's discovery did not, however, give rise to the development of a scientific model, since there was no broad cultural framework to receive and support it. Such insights usually collapsed under the weight of the primitive worldview in which they emerged. For Pierre Thuillier, professor of epistemology and the history of science, and Pierre Chaunu, one of the fathers of quantitative history, there is no question: The Judeo-Christian religion provided the basic architecture for developing a worldview that could effectively support the scientific model.

If one assumes that the Genesis text in fact reflects ultimate reality, what does it mean for the way we understand the supernatural?

First, magic as portrayed in the Harry Potter books or on innumerable websites devoted to witchcraft and the occult, simply does not exist. By magic, I do not mean conjuring tricks such as those performed by David Copperfield, or the romantic feeling we associate with a special event

---

15   In that same vein, Christopher Kaiser's comment is worth noting. He writes: "An operational faith in God as creator was a vital factor in the development of all branches of science until the late eighteenth century" (*Creation and the History of Science* [London: Marshall Pickering; Grand Rapids, MI: Eerdmans, 1991], 273).

such as the "magic" of Christmas. I am referring to the belief that there is some kind of supernatural/paranormal power or a web of cosmic energy that can be manipulated by psychics. The cosmological model presented in Genesis 1 obliterates the conditions necessary to postulate the reality of magic or the validity of paranormal phenomena.

Allow me to clarify further. I do not suggest supernatural phenomena have never occurred. There have been such occurrences in the past and there will no doubt be more in the future. But I contend that these events are caused by God who alone has the authority and power to effect real supernatural phenomena in human history. Satan, demons, demon worshipers, Hindu gurus, Voodoo priests and New Age psychics have no real power whatsoever. Their only powers are those of illusion, deceit and persuasion.

Throughout the Bible, there are various allusions to supernatural events. The Ten Plagues of Egypt, Moses' rod, Samuel talking from the land of the dead, a hand writing on the wall in the book of Daniel, Jesus' miracles, the apostles' deliverance from jail in Acts 5, etc. But a close examination of these incidents will demonstrate that God was the source in every instance. The biblical text portrays every other instance of "magic" as illusion.

Moses's encounter with Pharaoh is a good case in point. In Egypt where there was a long tradition of illusionist arts ("their secret arts," Exod. 7:11), the magicians could only imitate Moses's acts of power on a very small scale.[16] For instance, transforming the magicians' staffs into snakes was probably an illusionist's trick. L. Keimer suggests that the Egyptian cobra could be immobilized by applying pressure to the muscles at the nape of the neck. The serpents were charmed, then seized at the neck—as shown on several scarab-amulets—and thus temporarily immobilized. When the magician released it, it would regain muscle control and transform into a snake.[17] That the magicians really had no effective power was demonstrated when, in the end, Aaron's staff swallowed up the magicians' (Exod. 7:12).

From a theoretical standpoint, the Genesis 1 portrait of the universe obliterates the framework necessary for magic. It effectively neutralizes the very possibility of occult powers and paranormal phenomena, such as those depicted in popular television shows such as the "X-Files," "Buffy the Vampire

---

16   See for example Exod. 7:22-25; 8:7-14.

17   See L. Keimer, *Histoires de serpents dans L'Egypte ancienne et moderne* (Cairo, 1947), 16-17.

Slayer" and "Heroes." Genesis 1 contradicts all claims to supernatural powers, including those who pretend to control objects by the power of the mind, predict the future, levitate or have access to a mystical web of psychic energy. The claims made by occult practitioners, eastern gurus or New Age adherents presuppose a web of psychic energy that can be manipulated through a variety of occult techniques.[18] The Creation account's opening verse leaves no room for such. It also undermines any notion that objects or places can have inherent occult powers.

Some readers may wonder how I can be so categorical in challenging the reality of all supernatural phenomena. How can anyone really know? Isn't it preposterous to claim there are no occult powers when there seems to be so much evidence to the contrary? This is a fair question, and I would like to offer two reasons to support my statement.

One, this affirmation is based on an authoritative theoretical statement, i.e., Genesis 1. If the Creation account reflects absolute reality, then magic is impossible. It's just as in science: If the theory is sound, it will always pan out in experiments. Engineers do not have to go through a process of trial and error to build a bridge strong enough to support its own weight and that of rush hour traffic. I admit that I have not personally investigated every supernatural claim ever made. And frankly, I don't believe I need to. If the premises are sound, the conclusions will also be sound. Even those who do not believe in the Scripture's divine inspiration would do well to consider its extremely successful track record; there is more than ample reason to give it the benefit of the doubt.

Some readers will nevertheless insist that there are people who have supernatural powers. Perhaps! But this is easier to say than to prove. James Randi has devoted over three decades of his life to verifying supernatural claims. Earlier on, Randi chose to quit his career as a magician because people actually believed he had real powers. He was so concerned with his audience's gullibility and the general rise of irrational thinking in Western society, that he created the James Randi Educational Foundation. Not only does Randi investigate all kinds of supernatural claims, but his organization

---

18   For more details, see Antoine Faivre, "What is Occultism?" in *Hidden Truths. Magic, Alchemy, and the Occult*, ed. by Lawrence E. Sullivan (New York, NY: MacMillan, 1989 [1987]), 3-96.

offers a one-million-dollar prize to anyone who can show—under proper observing conditions—evidence of any paranormal, supernatural or occult power or event such as moving objects through the power of the mind, predicting the future, reading thoughts, levitating, etc. Not only has Randi successfully debunked various occult claims over the years, but that million dollars has been sitting in the bank since 1996 and it is still there as I write these lines![19] In spite of the widespread reports of real supernatural powers or events, the reality always seems to be a case of the man who saw the man who saw the bear!

What You See is What you Get! (Gen. 1:2-25)

Genesis 1:2-25 contains a number of statements that further clarify the highly dense opening affirmation of verse 1.

First, unlike the Mesopotamian myths, the Creation process in Genesis 1 reveals no sign of war, violence or struggle. The waters, the vegetation, the sun, the moon and the stars came simply into being by virtue of God's agency. God is portrayed as having absolute sovereignty over all the elements of nature. God spoke and it happened.

In that respect, the references to the creation of the "Seas" in verse 10 and the "great sea monsters" in verse 21 are remarkable. In ancient Mesopotamia, the seas represented the primordial chaos that constantly threatened to overwhelm the earth. In the *Enuma Elish*, we read that after Marduk vanquished the goddess Tiamat—a chaos monster—and used her various body parts to create the world, he had to post guards to keep "her waters," upon which the earth rested, from escaping.[20] In the Sumerian *Epic of Gilgamesh*, the hero Enkidu had to vanquish the dragon-like sea monster Huwawa. In other stories, the water god Enki waged war against the personified primal waters that threatened to overwhelm him.[21] And in Canaanite literature, the chief Canaanite deity Baal had to battle the sea monster Yam, also known as Lotan or "Leviathan" in the Old Testament, who was attempting to impose his rule.[22]

---

19   For more information, the reader can consult the James Randi Educational Foundation's website at http://www.randi.org/.

20   Boyd discusses this theme at length in *God at War*, 73-92.

21   Boyd, *God at War*, 78.

22   Boyd, *God at War*, 79.

In the Genesis story, the "seas" come into being by God's action. Far from being a threat, they are said to be "good" (v. 10). The mention of the "sea creatures" in verse 21 emphasizes that they are not menacing powers of chaos, but creatures over which God has absolute authority.[23] In that verse, the author explicitly drains the sea and its creatures of any divine or otherwise supernatural attributes the Canaanites and ancient Mesopotamians believed they had: "So God created the great sea monsters and every living creature that moves, of every kind, with which the waters swarm,..."

Verses 11-12 eliminate any correlation between vegetation and a god of nature, such as the Canaanite Baal or Ishtar in the Mesopotamian pantheon. In this text, Elohim is the creator of the plants and trees; therefore he is the one who grants fertility. In verse 12, as Gordon Wenham points out, not only does God create various kinds of plants, but he also gives them the power to reproduce.[24] This ability for plants and trees to reproduce themselves is intrinsic to the way God created the universe. Fertility does not depend on human efforts to please the gods; the power to reproduce is already written into the very DNA of every plant. In normal conditions, humans can take fertility for granted. It is not something they have to beg or bargain for.

The creation of the sun, the moon and the stars in verses 14-19 represents one of the most extraordinary aspects of this chapter. Ancient Mesopotamians worshiped the heavenly bodies because they believed them to be reflections of living deities.

Ancient astrologers attributed a twofold significance to the sun, moon and stars. First, their movements reflected mythological events in the lives of the gods. For example, the Babylonians saw manifestations of the moon-god Sin and his battles with other deities in the various phases of the moon. Second, the heavenly bodies pointed to a greater framework that reflected eternal and immutable laws and in which the gods lived out their lives.[25] The fate of the entire world and the destiny of every individual were under the irresistible control of the stars.

The statements in verses 14-19 contrast sharply with ancient Near Eastern beliefs. Our text describes the heavenly bodies as part of the created order.

---

23   See also Psalm 74:13; Isaiah 27:1.

24   See Wenham, *Genesis 1-15*, 21.

25   For more details, see Y. Kaufmann, *The Religion of Israel*, 46-48.

Just like everything else, they come into being as a result of God's creative word. These bodies are stripped of any divine character; they become mere objects. They no longer hold sway over human destiny and have absolutely no power over the fate of the world. They are simply created to mark the times! *"…and let them be for signs and for seasons and for days and years"* (v. 14).

The sun and the moon are created to give light, period! There is no hint whatsoever in the text that these heavenly objects are any more than they appear to be, i.e., cosmic light bulbs! As Gerhard von Rad has so aptly said: "The expression 'lights' and 'lamps' is meant to be prosaic and degrading."[26] To add insult to injury, these celestial objects are not even creators of light; because light was present prior to their creation (see Gen 1:3-5)! At best, they are the "mediating bearers of a light."[27] The great Old Testament scholar, Claus Westermann, adds: "The utter creatureliness of the heavenly bodies has never before been expressed in such revolutionary terms, as far as we know."[28] In the perspective of this text, one cannot imagine a more ridiculous practice than to set up worship shrines for these celestial objects or to consult their movements to determine the future. The injunctions against worshiping the sun, the moon and the stars found in Deuteronomy (4:19; 17:3) or the deriding comments of Isaiah (47:13) and Jeremiah (10:2-5) profoundly reflect the demythologized perspective of the Creation account.

The author goes to great lengths to undermine pagan beliefs. Many scholars note, for example, that the text does not use the usual terminology to denote the sun and the moon. Instead, the author uses the unusual "greater light" and "lesser light." This may have been done deliberately to avoid any confusion between these celestial objects and the deities they were supposed to represent.[29]

Much more could be said, but one thing emerges clearly. According to Genesis 1, the physical universe is utterly without consciousness. The material

---

26   See Gerhard von Rad, *Genesis*, rev. ed. (Philadelphia, PA: Westminster, 1972 [1961], 55.

27   Von Rad, *Genesis*, 56.

28   Claus Westermann, *Creation* (Fortress Press, 1974), 44.

29   Victor P. Hamilton notes that the normal expressions for sun and moon were, in Semitic languages, the names of divinities (*The Book of Genesis: Chapters 1-17*, NICOT [Grand Rapids, MI: Eerdmans, 1990], 127-128).

world does not contain esoteric knowledge that can only be discovered through the agency of some guru, astrologer or diviner. There is no cosmic or divinely ordered destiny in the stars, in animal organs or in the movements of migratory animals.[30] Genesis 1 states in no uncertain terms that human destiny is not contingent upon mysterious divine cosmic powers.

In terms of contemporary implications, Genesis 1 effectively negates the reality of occult and magical powers. This text administers a mortal blow to every supernatural claim imaginable: astrology, tarot card reading, crystal ball gazing, dowsing, communicating with the dead, etc. If we take it seriously, we must conclude that there is no magical force that can be controlled by means of some occult science accessible only to a few initiates and available for a steep price.

Genesis 1 is shocking by its simplicity: The sun was created to provide light during the day, and the stars and the moon to provide light at night. What you see is what you get! The author of this text wanted to portray the universe as a friendly place for humanity.

The Power at the Helm of the Universe

"Now the earth was formless and empty, darkness was over the surface of the deep, and the Spirit of God was hovering over the waters" (Gen. 1:2-NIV).

Though the Creation account author goes to great lengths to strip the physical universe of its mythological moorings, the text does not reflect a deistic perception of God. The great theologian does not attempt to portray the universe as a kind of mechanism which, like a wound clock, is left to unwind on its own with no outside intervention. While it has never been necessary to postulate the necessity of divine intervention to explain any empirical phenomenon, the Bible nevertheless vigorously affirms the reality of God's presence and his power to intervene in human history.

This principle is repeatedly illustrated throughout Israel's history. It is powerfully affirmed in the incarnation of Jesus Christ and again in the promise of the Holy Spirit to the Church. While God's existence cannot

---

30   For more information on divination in ancient Mesopotamia, see particularly A. Leo Oppenheim, *Ancient Mesopotamia*, rev. ed. (Chicago, IL: The University of Chicago Press, 1977 [1964]), 206-227.

be empirically proven, Genesis 1:2b is nevertheless a powerful statement affirming the reality of God's presence in the world. While Genesis 1:1 dissolves the mythical world of the ancient Near East by pointing to the reality of one single deity who creates all, the allusion to the Spirit of God, *ruach elohim*, in Gen 1:2b points, right from the outset, to the real nature of the ultimate power that governs the universe and clarifies its relationship to humanity.

At the Pinpoint Origin of the Universe (Gen. 1:2)

"...*and the Spirit of God was hovering over the waters*" (Gen. 1:2 NIV). Why does the author refer to the Spirit of God at this point in the text? First of all, it has to do with the author's magnificent communication skills. The reference to the Spirit in a text designed to provide the foundations for a new worldview is very strategic. The great theologian is not only attempting to capture the minds of the Israelites, it is important to him that he also reach and win their hearts.

The word for "Spirit" is the Hebrew word *ruach*, which can mean both "wind" and "spirit." While the context normally clarifies the word's exact meaning,[31] in this case, scholars have been uncertain about how to accurately interpret it. Though some scholars translate the expression *ruach elohim* as "a mighty wind,"[32] based on the normal meaning of the expression "Spirit of God," it is preferable to follow the more traditional reading. As Wenham points out, it is very unlikely that "Elohim" would be used as a superlative in this context. In addition, wherever the phrase *ruach elohim* is used in the Old Testament, it always denotes some manifestation of God.[33]

In the setting of a text that seeks to provide a new frame of reference to describe God and his relationship to humanity, *ruach* very likely plays double duty. If on the one hand, the allusion to "Spirit" was to reflect the personal

---

31 For a detailed study of the word *ruach*, see M. V. Van Pelt, W. C. Kaiser, and D. I. Block, "x;Wr," *New International Dictionary of Old Testament Theology and Exegesis*, ed. by W. A. VanGermeren, vol. 5 (Grand Rapids, MI: Zondervan, 1997), 1073-1078.

32 See for instance, Claus Westermann, *Genesis 1-11*, tr. by John J. Scullion (Minneapolis, MN: Augsburg Publishing House, 1984 [1974]), 107-108. For more details, see Wenham, *Genesis 1-15*, 16.

33 See Wenham, *Genesis 1-15*, 17.

character of God, on the other hand, the "wind" represented a symbolic allusion to this power. In his book, *Hermeneutical Spiral*, Grant Osborne reminds the reader that there is no necessity to read only one meaning into any one word. In some cases, words can simultaneously refer to two realities. Although one may not want to make the opposite error of reading every possible meaning of a word into a specific passage, in some contexts the author may have intended for more than one meaning to be understood.[34] That we should read "wind" in addition to the personal "Spirit" is highly plausible since ancient Near Eastern people were generally familiar with the concept of the wind as a primordial power. Unlike the wind of Genesis 1:2, the winds of the ancient myths embodied forces of violence and anarchy;[35] they announced humanity's slavery and symbolized terror and ill fortune.

The great theologian was well aware of the necessity to redefine the universe's primal force. But the "wind/spirit" is not quite what the average reader would expect. Unlike the mythology of the time, this wind had nothing to do with violence, destruction or war. The *ruach* Elohim is associated with peace, serenity and tranquility. Far from being an anonymous and destructive force and the source of anguish and chaos, this wind was a source of reassurance. Whenever *ruach* was linked to the name of God—Elohim—it was no longer simply the wind. It took characteristics of personality as well, becoming the "wind of God," the Spirit of God. The universe was no longer the unfathomable infinite and chaotic cosmos that made humans feel so puny and insignificant. There was no blind fate at the helm. At the pinpoint origin of the universe, there was a person. There was reason, heart and compassion. There was no longer any justification for harboring an irrational fear of the primordial force in the universe.

And the Spirit of God was hovering over the Waters (Gen. 1:2 NIV)

For many readers, the image of the Spirit "hovering" will seem somewhat disconcerting. For some, "hovering" may even entail negative connotations. Such a word may evoke images of UFOs, alien abductions or some other ominous threat. For others, the notion of something hovering is simply too vague to be meaningful.

---

34 See Grant Osborne, *The Hermeneutical Spiral* (Downers Grove, IL: InterVarsity Press, 1991), 74.

35 See *Enuma Elish*, Tablet 4, and Atrahasis, *Tablet II*.

For starters, the Hebrew verb has no negative connotations at all. Although it is not an easy word to translate, the intent of the Hebrew verb *rachaph* is clear in Deuteronomy 32:11, the only other place the verb is used in this form (*piel*). The Deuteronomy passage evokes the protective image of the eagle that "hovers over its young." Likewise, Genesis 1:2 does not describe some evil power brooding over the yet-unformed universe. On the contrary, it projects an image of warmth and intimacy. Think of parents who bring their newborn child over to the house for the first time and who literally "hover" over the child: observing, listening, marveling at their baby, ready to offer their lives to protect this most vulnerable of all creatures.

The power that governs the universe is not hostile to humanity. It is not bent on destruction. That power loves and cares for creation. It is a loud proclamation from the very heart of God: "Take heart! You are not alone!" Evil, fate and chance do not ultimately define human reality. The force that regulates the universe is both personal and powerful. The Spirit of God watches over the world.

Genesis 1:2 also proclaims that the Spirit is active. The Spirit is not some cloaked and uncaring entity that can only be found through elaborate rituals and sacrifices. This Spirit announces the coming action of a God who has a benevolent intent for all. The author offers his audience what men and women need the most: hope.

Viktor Frankle, a professor of psychiatry at the University of Vienna, spent three years at Auschwitz and other Nazi prisons. In his book, *Man's Search for Meaning*, he wrote about the absolute necessity of having hope to survive the horrendous conditions prisoners experienced in the concentration camps. When such hope would evaporate, survival became nearly impossible: "The prisoner who had lost faith in the future—his future—was doomed. With his loss of belief in the future, he also lost his spiritual hold; he let himself decline and became subject to mental and physical decay."[36] Often, it is not the problems themselves that do us in.

---

36 Viktor E. Frankl, Man's Search for Meaning, rev. ed. (New York, NY: Pocket Books, 1963 [1959]), 117.

A person does not just give up on a spouse out of the blue. When people consider leaving their marriage, it is often because they have given up hope that things can change. When a man considers ending his own life, it is because there is no hope left. The conviction that the Spirit of God hovers over creation and is intensely concerned about our lives will create a profound sense of hope, for it is the assurance that there is a greater power at work in us.

One of human nature's great pitfalls is that we tend to think of ourselves as the center of the world. To a great extent, this is not surprising. Not only are we self-centered by nature, we also physically perceive the world with everything in orbit around each one of us. But this is only an illusion. None of us is the center of the world. This misperception of reality is shattered every time we are the victims of a major tragedy. When we are struck by misfortune—cancer, the loss of a loved one, financial ruin—we suddenly understand that we are not at the center of the universe, and the realization that we are just like everyone else hits us like a ton of bricks. While suffering may intensely captivate a man's full attention, millions of people simply continue to live their merry lives without giving him so much as a single thought. The worst thing about the imminence of death is that it reminds us that there is nothing special about any one of us. Death is the great equalizer.

For many people, this has a devastating effect because it cruelly undermines their own sense of personal worth and significance. The allusion to the loving work of the Spirit over humanity is a powerful reminder that, though we may not be the center of the universe, we are indeed in the center of God's love! The apostle John expresses a similar truth in his first epistle when he writes: "*In this is love, not that we loved God but that he loved us and sent his Son to be the atoning sacrifice for our sins. …By this we know THAT WE ABIDE IN HIM and he in us, because he has given us of his Spirit.*" (1 John 4:10, 13).

John's words remind us of the comforting reality that we live in the very heart of God, a deep echo of the truth of the allusion to God's Spirit hovering over the world.

The Nature of Humanity
In Partnership with God (Gen. 1:27-28; 2:15-17)

In the Mesopotamian world, humanity's creation results from a conflict between the gods. Human existence has little intrinsic significance and value beyond serving the gods as slaves. The destiny of men and women is in the hands of cosmic powers that are beyond human control. Arbitrary divine action governs every aspect of human life.[37]

Genesis 1:27-28, 2:15-17 and 3:1-24 provide a radically different picture of the role attributed to humanity and how it relates to the powers. Partnership, not slavery, is the defining concept to describe humanity's role in the world and its relationship to God. Genesis 1:27-28 states:

So God created humankind in his image, in the image of God he created them; male and female he created them. God blessed them, and God said to them, "Be fruitful and multiply, and fill the earth and subdue it; and have dominion over the fish of the sea and over the birds of the air and over every living thing that moves upon the earth."

The notion of God's image is central to capturing the concept of partnership. Opinions about what the image of God means have been far ranging.[38]   On one side of the spectrum, theologians traditionally and most commonly defined "image" and "likeness" in terms of those spiritual and mental abilities human beings share with the creator; such as intelligence, self-determination, free will, creativity, etc. On the other side, scholars have suggested that "image" primarily reflects humanity's role as God's representative in creation.

The second option more consistently agrees with verse 28, which explicitly associates "image" with the task of ruling and subduing; tasks that describe the exercise of kingly authority.[39] "God blessed them, and God said to them, 'Be fruitful and multiply, and fill the earth and subdue it; and have dominion over the fish of the sea and over the birds of the air and over every living thing that moves upon the earth'" (Gen. 1:28). Psalm 8 reflects a

---

37   See Jean Bottéro, *La plus vieille religion. En Mésopotamie*, Folio/histoire (Gamillard, 1998), 210.

38   For a basic survey and assessment of the positions, see Wenham, *Genesis 1-15*, 29-32.

39   For more details, see Willem A. M. Beuken, "The Human Person in the Vision of Genesis 1-3: A Synthesis of Contemporary Insights," *Louvain Studies* 24 (1999):3-20.

similar perspective: *"You have given them dominion over the works of your hands; you have put all things under their feet, all sheep and oxen, and also the beasts of the field, the birds of the air, and the fish of the sea, whatever passes along the paths of the seas"* (Ps. 8:6-8).

Genesis 2:15-17 further develops the principle found in Genesis 1:27-28:

> *The LORD God took the man and put him in the garden of Eden to till it and keep it. And the LORD God commanded the man, "You may freely eat of every tree of the garden; but of the tree of the knowledge of good and evil you shall not eat, for in the day that you eat of it you shall die."*

In verse 15, God takes the man and puts him in the Garden of Eden to work it and care for it. The significance of this text goes far beyond a divine mandate to take care of a plot of land. It primarily functions to address the universality of the human condition. This text is not just about Adam. It reflects an invitation for all people to enter into a cooperative relationship with the creator. Verses 16 and 17 provide the overall context and the parameters that will define the terms of the relationship. The image conveyed in these verses is not that of the slave, but of the partner who is given a mandate and the authority to fulfill it within the broader framework of God's intent.

Masters of Our Fate (Gen. 3:1-24)

Christians have historically highlighted, and with good reason, the negative aspects of humanity's Fall depicted in Genesis 3:1-24. While it is not my intent to lessen the horrific impact of that event on human nature and human history,[40] it is important to point out at least one positive aspect of this narrative.

Besides explaining the origins of human misery, Genesis 3 also provides an important reminder and affirmation that human beings are the masters of their own destiny. To grasp the full significance of that story, we need to keep Genesis 2:15-17 in close proximity. In Genesis 2:15-17, God offers a

---

40   For an interesting treatment of the account of the Fall, see Henri Blocher, *Original Sin*, New Studies in Biblical Theology (Grand Rapids, MI: Eerdmans, 1999).

choice to Adam—obey or disobey—with clear and explicit consequences tied to each option. Whereas obedience would bring life, disobedience would result in death.

Life and death are wisdom code words that refer to the type of existence human beings can choose for themselves. Genesis 2:15-17 teaches that human destiny is not determined by some external and irresistible force, but by the very choices that humans make. This perspective is announced in Genesis 2 and implemented in chapter 3, where Adam and Eve choose to disobey God's command and reap, in accordance with Genesis 2, the consequences of their actions. At this moment of critical choice, they are ushered into the age of pain, misery, violence and death.

As tragic as that may be, at the very least, this text confirms humanity's inherent dignity. In other words, free will cannot be considered in isolation; it goes hand in hand with the notion of human dignity. But dignity is not a commodity that flourishes in a vacuum. It is intrinsically linked to responsibility: the right to live with the consequences of one's actions. This is the true significance of human dignity. The message of Genesis 3 is unmistakable. Human beings are given the power to determine their own destiny regarding the kind of people they will become and the kind of world they will live in.

The good news of self-determination is a familiar theme in Scripture. For instance, it is foundational to the use of the blessing and the curse found throughout the Old Testament. Israel is repeatedly faced with the option of obeying or disobeying the demands of the covenant, with specific blessings and curses tagged to each alternative. The prophets consistently erupt on the scene when the people are in violation of the covenant's basic requirements. While we might have expected them to focus on the judgment they deserved, these men called the people to leave their rebellious ways and turn back to God.

The notion of self-determination is particularly prominent in biblical wisdom literature. The book of Proverbs, for instance, repeatedly affirms human self-determination and human dignity. The Old Testament scholar, Walter Brueggemann, suggests that biblical wisdom—echoing Genesis 2:15-17—fundamentally calls men and women to consider and embrace the *way of life*, an ideal of human existence that promotes life in all of its facets; the "well-being of the community and each of its members, i.e., *shalom*."[41]

Genesis 1-3 and the Demonic Warfare Worldview

I pointed out at the beginning of this chapter that the demonic warfare model advocated by Peter C. Wagner, John Dawson, Ed Murphy and others reflects many of the basic elements of the Canaanite/Mesopotamian worldview.

I am not suggesting that these leaders intentionally borrowed from Mesopotamian ideology. If only! In reality, it's much more subtle than that. Human societies have an innate tendency to reproduce, generation after generation, what I call ideological structures of death: i.e., ideologies that promote war and violence as a basic characteristic of human existence and, on a deeper level, ideologies that continually recreate structures of dehumanization and human exploitation.

Human cultures throughout history have tended to reinvent, in ever-new forms, what I now call the "Old Myth."[42] The following elements represent some of the most prominent characteristics of the death ideology that erupts with every new generation.

- Violence as a founding principle
- Ethnocentricity
- Racial superiority
- Racism
- The divine at the service of the State
- Deification/worship of nature
- Belief in the power of magic
- Objectification of human nature/slavery

---

41 Walter Brueggemann, *In Man We Trust* (Richmond, VA: John Knox Press, 1972), 13-28.

42 I suspect Jesus' repeated warnings against the temptation to use the means of this "world," i.e., power and violence, constitute a profound allusion to the reality of this "Old Myth." John's references to the "world" also point to the presence of a persistent system of beliefs which ultimately produces death in human cultures (John 7:7; 1 John 2:15-16). One must also mention René Girard whose thesis on violence as a founding principle of human society and institutions has identified regular patterns of human behavior generalized in literature (see particularly *La violence et le sacré* [Paris: Grasset, 1972], *Des choses cachées depuis la fondation du monde* [Bernard Grasset, 1978], and *Le bouc émissaire* [Paris: Grasset, 1982]). In English, Girard's classic exposition of his thesis has been published under the title, *Violence and the Sacred*, tr. P. Gregory (Baltimore, MD: Johns Hopkins University Press, 1977). In addition, the reader may also consult *Deceit, Desire and the Novel: Self and Other in Literary Structure*, tr. by Y. Freccero (Baltimore, MD: Johns Hopkins University Press, 1965) and *The Scapegoat*, tr. by Y. Freccero (Baltimore, MD: Johns Hopkins University Press, 1989).

Today, for example, the Old Myth finds expression in the theory of evolution with its emphasis on violence and the notion of the "survival of the fittest/strongest." The New Age movement, with its focus on manipulating magical/cosmic powers and its reductionistic assimilation of human dignity and identity into the realm of nature, represents another expression of the Old Myth.

The Church is not immune. I submit that the wholehearted affirmation of the demonic warfare model represents another such expression of the Old Myth.

The Creation account was designed to provide an alternative to the Mesopotamian worldview. But, in as much as the Mesopotamian worldview reflected a universal ideology that fundamentally promoted death, dehumanization and oppression, I suggest that the creation account did not simply offer an alternative to the ancient Canaanite/Mesopotamian worldview, but also critiqued the ideology human cultures tend to default to. If the demonic warfare model reflects the basic tenets of the Old Myth, then it follows that Genesis 1-3 can and should be used to evaluate that ideology, particularly as it pertains to some of its most important assumptions, such as its perception of how the physical universe and demonic entities interact, the unconscious demonization of people, the magical connection between demon-possession and traumatic violence, and the alleged utter vulnerability of humans to demonic influence.

In order to show as clearly as possible the contrast between the biblical worldview and the demonic warfare model, I will now summarize the implications that derive from Genesis 1-3.[43]

- The universe is created good by a benevolent God. The universe is ordered, predictable and meaningful. The environment is not something to fear, it is the very expression of a generous God.

- The creation of the universe originates in the intention of a good God; not in a primordial, violent, cosmic conflict.

---

43   It is interesting to note that in his brilliant analysis of biblical wisdom, Brueggemann discerns similar themes. For example, the notion of a fundamentally friendly universe is central to biblical wisdom. For more details, see In Man We Trust, 14-28.

- Human beings are created with fundamental dignity and basic freedom with respect to God.

- Human beings are responsible for their actions.

- Human fate is in the hands of God, but also in our capacity to choose that which leads to life or death.

- Sin and its results are the consequences of human choice. Sin affects our humanity and our human existence, however, it does not rob us of our basic human dignity and our ability to choose God (see Gen. 4:6-7).

- Human beings are called to embrace life.

- Human beings are created to be in partnership with God. Humanity is given the mandate to be God's "image," i.e., to represent the sovereign God on the earth. Men and women are expected to be in constant consultation with God. This consultation must be present at all levels of human experience, such as discerning our role in God's project, and appealing for special strength and wisdom in times of crisis. In the Creation account, dialog with God is the response to life's challenges.

The following table contrasts the Mesopotamian and Demonic Warfare worldviews with the basic tenets of creation theology:

A Comparative Outline of Three Worldviews

Mesopotamian	Demonic Warfare	Creation Account
Creation originates in violence.	Humanity's creation is set against a backdrop of conflict and war.	Creation originates in peace and God's benevolent intention.
The universe is mythologized.	The universe is mythologized.	The universe is demythologized.
The gods' malevolent influence is mediated through the environment.	The demons' malevolent influence is mediated through the environment.	Negates the possibility of magic. The primordial "power" (Spirit of God) is good.

Mesopotamian	Demonic Warfare	Creation Account
The gods operate within a highly organized hierarchy.	Demons operate within a highly organized hierarchy.	There is only one God.
Human experience is characterized by conflict with the gods.	The Christian experience is characterized by conflict with demonic powers.	The human experience is defined as a partnership with God.
Human experience is characterized by fear and uncertainty.	The Christian experience is characterized by fear and uncertainty.	Human experience is characterized by knowledge and confidence.
Human fate is contingent on the gods.	The Christian is constantly living under the possible influence of the demonic world.	Human fate is contingent on a relationship with God.
People are dependent on diviners to exorcize their world.	Christians are dependent on spiritual warfare "specialists" to exorcize their world.	There is no need to exorcize the universe.

The Creation account teaches that humans inhabit a friendly universe in which they can live with confidence, joy and certainty. I do not deny the risks and challenges inherent to this world. Human beings do face a wide range of difficulties, but they are lodged in the realm of reason, not magic. The notion of a universe supported by a "net" of occult forces mysteriously affecting human beings or manipulated by them—as depicted in numerous movies and television series—is entirely foreign to the Creation account. Any ideology, Christian or non-Christian, which assumes the existence of such a net flies squarely in the face of Creation theology.

But what about demons? Do they exist? Do they influence us? Or are they simply projections of the human subconscious? Certainly not! Both the Old and New Testaments confirm the existence of these nasty beings from hell.

Then what? How can we reconcile the reality of these beings with what Genesis 1-3 teaches about the world we live in? This is what the next chapter will explore. I will demonstrate that there are, in fact, no contradictions between what the New Testament and Genesis 1-3 teach about demons. The issue does not revolve around whether these beings exist or not, but around the way human and demonic spheres interact with one another.

Chapter 3:

A Biblical Theology of Spiritual Warfare

Introduction

In the last chapter, I proposed that the way demons and Satan are most often perceived in religious circles today reflects an ideology that has more in common with the old Mesopotamian worldview than with biblical theology. Am I implying that Satan and demonic beings either do not exist or pose no threat to human beings? Hardly! Since the New Testament hints very strongly at the reality of demonic beings that struggle against God and his kingdom, it would be foolhardy to ignore this dimension of spiritual reality. How then do we reconcile the notion of a friendly universe as proposed in Genesis 1-3 with the New Testament portrayal of hostile demonic powers?

The main issue is not about scientifically proving the existence of demons or Satan. This is impossible! Instead, we must focus on whether or not Scripture confirms the existence of such beings, and how it portrays the mode of interaction between demons and humans. If Peretti, Wagner, Dawson and Murphy's portrayal of spiritual reality is accurate, then we better get on with the program: We should seek the protection of spiritual warfare specialists, and earnestly and constantly utter prayers of protection to create a "spiritual shield" against these malevolent beings. There is no middle way! Either we live in a universe that is under siege from "spiritual terrorists" against whom we should immunize ourselves, or else we live in a friendly universe.

If demons do exist and interact with human beings, what is the framework that allows such an interaction? And what is the precise nature of that interaction? Intuitively, most people assume that it occurs in a fashion akin to magic or the occult. But the Creation account provides no support whatsoever to maintain this assumption.

In addressing these critical and controversial issues, I have deliberately chosen to rely on relevant biblical material. Demonic warfare specialists have a tendency to give predominance to experience, personal anecdotes and personal words of revelation (the *rhema* word). While I do not suggest they intentionally exclude Scripture, their interpretation clearly hinges on a theological system constructed from "field experience."

This chapter will explore three questions:

1. What biblical evidence supports the belief that Satan and demons are personal entities?

2. What can we say about the nature of these demonic beings?

3. How do they interact with human beings?

As I proceed to answer these questions, I will keep the worldview outlined in Genesis 1-3 as the basic backdrop. Concerning the reality of demonic activity, I will briefly survey the entire New Testament. Regarding the nature of the demonic and the character of their interaction with human beings, I will examine two texts that more intentionally target these matters: the Gospel of Mark and Paul's first letter to the Corinthians.[1]

The Reality of Demons

Whether demons or evil spirits really exist is an important question, but it cannot be scientifically resolved. To a large extent, the answer hinges on one's starting point. As with the broader issue of spiritual warfare, our position on whether demons exist or not will tend to grow out of the worldview we hold.

For instance, a secular worldview will not, by definition, acquiesce to the objective existence of evil beings or of one overarching devil who is bent on promoting evil throughout the world. Generally, secular academics perceive the devil either in psychological terms (i.e., as a projection of human evil or a symbol of psychological forces) or in anthropological terms (i.e., as the expression of a primitive worldview).[2] For true secularists, the mere suggestion that there might be some reality undergirding the notion of demons is inadmissible. Acknowledging the existence of a personal being like Satan would lead to the utter collapse of their worldview. Admitting the reality of satanic entities is simply not compatible with the underlying assumptions of secularism. But as a Christian theologian, I view the

---

1 The texts that will be examined will be interpreted on the basis of generally accepted hermeneutical principles. For more details, see for instance, Grant R. Osborne, *The Hermeneutical Spiral* (Downers Grove, IL: InterVarsity Press, 1991).

2 Jeffrey Burton Russell discusses the shift from belief in the devil as an objective reality to that of a psychological construct in *Mephistopheles: The Devil in the Modern World* (London: Cornell University Press, 1986), 262-264.

Bible—both the Old and the New Testaments—as divinely inspired. I believe that these texts, interpreted with due respect for their literary genres and their historical specificity, provide the foundation for articulating a worldview that reflects ultimate reality.

Although there are but few and ambiguous references to Satan and demons in the Old Testament,[3] the New Testament does, on the other hand, offer plenty of material to analyze. The existence of demons and of Satan is well documented in the New Testament.[4]

All three synoptic gospels report an encounter between Jesus and Satan right at the outset of Jesus' ministry (see Matt. 4:1-11; Mark 1:12-13; Luke 4:1-13). Although scholars have debated the historical character of these reports,[5] the Gospel writers portray this incident as a historical encounter between Jesus and a concrete being who sought to convince Jesus to accept a corrupt definition of his role as Messiah.[6] The Gospel accounts portray Satan as much more than a simple personification of Jesus' doubts about his calling!

In the Beelzebub controversy recorded in Matthew 12:22-32, Mark 3:20-30 and Luke 11:14-26, Jesus assumes the reality of Satan and his demons.[7] Three different parables contain a number of unambiguous references to the devil. When Jesus interprets the Parable of the Sower (Matt. 13:1-9; Mark 4:1-9; Luke 8:4-8), Satan[8] is identified as the agent symbolized by the birds. In his interpretation of the Parable of the Weeds, which only appears in Matthew 13:24-30, Jesus identifies the weeds as "the sons of the evil ones" (13:38) and the one who sows them as "the devil" (13:39). The Parable of the Sheep and the Goats (Matt. 25:31-46)

---

3 For more details on Satan in the Old Testament, see Page, *Powers of Evil*, 11-42.

4 For a detailed discussion of the demonic in the New Testament, see *Powers of Evil*, 87-265.

5 The issue is specifically linked to the literary genre of the accounts. These reports have for example been variously identified as myth, a haggadish Midrash, or a dramatization of a struggle in the mind of Jesus. See U. W. Mauser, *Christ in the Wilderness*, Studies in Biblical Theology, 1st series, no. 39 (London: SCM, 1963) and B. Gerhardsson, *The Testing of God's Son*, tr. by J. Toy, Coniectanea Biblica, New Testament, no. 2: fascicle 1 (Lund: Gleerup, 1966).

6 For a helpful discussion of the temptation of Jesus, see Page, *Powers of Evil*, 88-99.

7 For a detailed discussion of this incident, see Page, *Powers of Evil*, 99-109.

8 The three synoptic gospels use different titles to refer to Satan. Matthew speaks of the "evil one" (13:19), Mark uses "Satan" (4:15), and Luke refers to "the devil" (8:12).

includes a reference to the eternal fire which was prepared for the "devil and his angels" (Matt. 25:41).

On at least four occasions, Jesus exorcised people who were said to be "demon-possessed."

1. Mark 1:21-28 and Luke 4:33-37 report the case of the demon-possessed man in the Capernaum synagogue.

2. Matthew 8:28-34, Mark 5:20 and Luke 8:26-39 record the case of the Gerasenes demoniac (or demoniacs according to Matthew).

3. Matthew 15:21-28 and Mark 7:24-30 tell the deliverance story of the Syrian Phoenician woman's daughter. According to both accounts, this woman went to Jesus because her daughter was possessed by "an unclean spirit" (Mark 7:25). Matthew quotes the woman as saying her daughter is "tormented by a demon" (15:22). Matthew does not explicitly corroborate the woman's "diagnosis." He simply states that her daughter was healed. In Mark's version, Jesus confirms that the demon left.

4. The account of the epileptic boy found in the synoptic gospels (Matt. 17:14-20; Mark 9:14-29; Luke 9:37-43) represents the fourth major exorcism in which Jesus was involved. While in Matthew, the father makes no allusion to any evil spirit, Mark and Luke record the man's explicit allusion to the presence of a demon as the cause of the son's illness. In all three gospels, Jesus rebukes the evil spirit and the child is healed. When in Matthew and Mark, the disciples inquire about their failure to help the child, Jesus comments on the reasons for their inability to chase the demon.

There are additional references to demonic beings in the gospels, but the preceding examples will suffice for now. John's Gospel contains no references to evil spirits as such, but we do find a number of allusions to the devil. In 8:44, he is the "murderer" and the "father of lies." Jesus refers to the "ruler of this world" in 12:31, 14:30 and 16:11.

The book of Acts includes three major references to demons. In the first two (Acts 5:16; 8:5-8), Luke provides a summary statement about the ministry of the apostles and Philip respectively. In Acts 5:16, Luke reports that the crowds brought their sick and "those tormented by unclean spirits."

In 8:5-8, the author records that evil spirits came out of many. In both of these texts, the physician Luke distinguishes between those who are demon-possessed and those who simply suffer from an illness. This is an important observation since it is often said that, at the time of Jesus, people indiscriminately confused all cases of illness with demon-possession. This was just not the case.

Acts 16:16-18 records the only detailed case of an exorcism involving a slave girl "who had a spirit of divination." At some point, the girl began to harass Paul and those who were with him. After a few days, Paul rebuked the spirit and it immediately left her. After the exorcism, we learn that the girl could no longer perform her divining duties, and thus ceased to be a source of income for her owners (Acts 16:19).

The epistles also contain important references to Satan and demons. In 2 Corinthians 4:4, Satan is called the "god of this world" who keeps people from receiving the illumination of the Gospel. In Ephesians 6:10-20, Paul exhorts his readers to put on the armor of God and refers to the "wiles of the devil" against believers.

Satan is sometimes described as one who seeks opportunities to tempt human beings. In Ephesians 4:26-27, Paul tells the readers to avoid giving the devil a foothold through anger. In 1 Corinthians 7:5, sexual abstinence can become an opportunity for Satan to tempt men and women (see also 1 Timothy 5:14-15). In 2 Corinthians 2:5-11, Paul emphasizes the importance of forgiving and comforting a repentant person who has been found in sin; failure to do so could leave opportunity for Satan to scheme against the community. Second Corinthians 11:14 accuses Satan of masquerading as an angel of light.[9] In Romans 16:20, Paul speaks of the victory over Satan God gives to believers.

Second Thessalonians 2:9-10 mentions Satan in connection with the revelation of the "lawless one." The book of Hebrews mentions the devil only once in 2:14, in connection with the purpose of Christ's death: "...so that through death he might destroy the one who has the power of death, that is, the devil, and free those who all their lives were held in slavery by the fear of death."

---

9 It should be noted that these passages do not underscore the ontological reality of Satan in the same way as some of the other passages I have alluded to. It remains important , however, to include them both to show the semantic range of the word Satan and to underline the ethical and ideological character of spiritual warfare (see also Page, *Powers of Evil*, 189).

First John contains more references to the devil than any of the other non-Pauline letters. Those who are unregenerate are described as "children of the devil" (1 John 3:8,10). The whole world is under the control of the evil one (5:19). For John, the purpose of the incarnation was to destroy the devil's work (3:8). He addresses the "young people" as having overcome the evil one (2:13-14). In 4:4, readers are assured that they have overcome those who sought to convince them to accept false teaching *"for the one who is in you is greater than the one who is in the world."* In 5:18, John states that the evil one cannot harm those who are born of God.

James, in his epistle, exhorts his readers to resist the devil. The assumption is that such resistance will be successful (James 4:7). For his part, Peter encourages believers to remain alert, knowing that *"the devil prowls around, looking for someone to devour"* (1 Peter 5:8-9).

Satan is mentioned more often in Revelation than in any other book of the Bible. The Arch-villain receives some attention in the letters to the seven churches: Smyrna (Rev. 2:9), Pergamum (2:13), Thyatira (2:24) and Philadelphia (3:9). There is possibly a reference to the devil in the account of the fifth trumpet in chapter 9:1-11, but the exact identity of the star and of the angel is uncertain.[10] In the series of heavenly visions found in chapter 12, Satan occupies a central place. In 16:13-14, John describes the emergence of three evil spirits that came out of the mouths of the "dragon," the "beast," and the "false prophet." Revelation 20 provides the picture of an angel binding Satan and locking him into the "bottomless pit" for a thousand years (vv. 1-3). In verses 7-10, Satan is once again given the power to deceive, but he is finally thrown into the lake of "fire and sulphur." [11]

Summary

This brief survey highlights the following elements about the demonic in the New Testament:

1) Satan and the demons are perceived as real beings. This stands, even though the expressions "Satan" or "devil" are not always used to denote a person, but sometimes a system or a principle that is in opposition to God.

---

10 See Sydney Page, *Powers*, 212.

11 For a more detailed discussion of these passages, refer to Sydney Page, *Powers of Evil*, 183-221.

2) Demonic powers exercise their influence over humanity in general and the Christian community in particular.

3) Satan attacks by tempting, afflicting and accusing human beings. The temptation to commit sin is most often mentioned.[12]

4) Satan and demons are mentioned in conjunction with illness (Paul's thorn in the flesh) and persecution.

The Authority and Power of Demons

If we follow the New Testament and assume the reality of demonic entities, how then do we characterize their interaction with human beings? Do these beings have real powers? And if so, how are they mediated?

We need to admit that these questions are, in the end, impossible to answer either philosophically or empirically. Even if we assume that demonic presence can be detected or otherwise signaled by some radical manifestation of evil, the reality is that it is virtually impossible to establish a direct relationship of cause and effect between a particular expression of evil and demonic spirits. Evil, at least from our vantage point, is always mediated by some historical process. Even such horrendous and unquestionably evil acts as those committed by the Paul Bernardo/Karla Homolka duo or by the so-called BTK serial killer, Dennis Rader, cannot be traced back to some supernatural evil being. The only agents we can unmistakably identify in the raping and killing spree that they engaged in are the individuals themselves.[13] Ultimately, the answer to whether or not such acts of radical evil are the product of demonic influence or not lies in our presuppositions; in other words, the worldview we adopt as authoritative.

Demonic warfare writers work under the assumption that the mode of interaction between the demonic and human spheres is magical in character. They assume the underlying reality of the occult and the reliability of the

---

12   Sydney Page, *Powers of Evil*, 220.

13   Those who may not be familiar with the horrible details of the Bernardo/Homolka case may want to consult: Scott Burnside and Alan Cairns, *Deadly Innocence. The True Story of Paul Bernardo,Karla Homolka, and the Schoolgirl Murders* (New York, NY: Warner Books, 1995); Nick Pron, *Lethal Marriage. The Unspeakable Crimes of Paul Bernardo and Karla Homolka* (New York, NY: Ballantine Books, 1996); Stephen Williams, *Invisible Darkness* (Bantam, 1997). Marilyn Bardsley offers a summary of the case in "Paul Bernardo and Karla Homolka," Crime Library, http://www.crimelibrary.com/serials/bernardo/bernmain.htm (accessed November 21, 2004).

countless stories that circulate about the supernatural. And they tend to read Scripture in light of these assumptions.

In the previous chapter, I made the case for using the Genesis Creation account as a starting point of our discussion. Genesis 1-3 states that God created humanity to live with meaning and significance in what is described as a friendly universe. If we take seriously what this text says, then how do we reconcile a "friendly" universe with the demonic powers in the New Testament?

The Gospel of Mark and 1 Corinthians 10-11 deal with one of the greatest fears of Gentiles and Jews alike: the fear of demonic powers. The Gospel of Mark is primarily addressed to a pagan audience that was characterized by a fear of the powers, be they divine or demonic. In 1 Corinthians 10-11, where Paul deals with the issue of meat sacrificed to idols, the apostle specifically addresses the relationship between demonic powers and human beings.

First century men and women in the Roman Empire would go to great lengths to immunize themselves against demonic powers. Graham H. Twelftree, in his important book, *Jesus the Exorcist*, writes: "… it was widely believed that the world was infested with beings hostile to man, against which protection or relief was sought."[14] Clinton E. Arnold, one of the foremost specialists on New Testament demonology further comments:

> The overriding characteristic of the practice of magic throughout the Hellenistic world was the cognizance of a spirit world exercising influence over virtually every aspect of life. The goal of the magician was to discern the helpful spirits from the harmful ones and learn the distinct operations and the relative strengths and authority of the spirits. Through this knowledge, means could be constructed (with spoken or written formulas, amulets, etc.) for the manipulation of the spirits in the interest of the individual person. With the proper formula, a spirit-induced sickness could be cured, a chariot race could be won, sexual passions could be enhanced, etc. Conversely, great harm could be brought to another person through the utterance of a curse.[15]

---

14   Graham H. Twelftree, *Jesus the Exorcist* (Peabody, MA: Hendrickson, 1993), 50.

15   Clinton E. Arnold, *Ephesians: Power and Magic* (Grand Rapids, MI: Baker, 1992 [1989]), 18.

Incidentally, this intense fear of demons—although quite manifest in the pagan world—was also present in the Jewish community. [16]

Jesus versus the Demonic in the Gospel of Mark

The Gospel of Mark mainly targets a Gentile audience, i.e., Christians who had converted from a pagan background. These people were mostly from the lower classes: the poor and slaves. Mark's audience was intensely preoccupied with the powers that they imagined filled the universe. They believed in magic and in the protection they could derive from various forms of magical practices. [17]

Fear of the demonic world was central in the use of magic. [18] We cannot underestimate how much daily life rotated around pleasing the gods and seeking protection against evil influences. Since part of Mark's agenda was to address some urgent issues relating to the devil and demons, his gospel will be helpful to survey.

Mark 1:12-13: *And the Spirit immediately drove him out into the wilderness. He was in the wilderness forty days, tempted by Satan; and he was with the wild beasts; and the angels waited on him.*

To understand the real significance of this passage, one must read it in the light of the parallel passages in Matthew and Luke. In contrast to Matthew 4:1-11 and Luke 4:1-13 where the encounter between Jesus and the devil is given significant space, Mark's Gospel only devotes one single verse to it. The text simply notes, "he [Jesus] was ...tempted by Satan." In this passage, Satan is, for all practical purposes, portrayed as an irrelevant quantity. He is present and he does tempt Jesus; but he is not a very significant actor and his action is devoid of impact.

In spite of the brevity of the reference, we should not underestimate its

---

16   See Graham H. Twelftree, *Christ Triumphant: Exorcism Then and Now* (London: Hodder and Stoughton, 1985), 25-54. Arnold has a very interesting discussion about the pervasive influence of magic and demonic interest in the Hellenistic world (see *Ephesians*, 14-40). On the subject of Jewish magic, see particularly Arnold's discussion (Ephesians, 31-34) and H. D. Betz, "Introduction to the Greek Magical Papyri, " *The Greek Magical Papyri in Translation* (Chicago, IL: University of Chicago Press, 1986), xlv.

17   See Clinton E. Arnold, *Ephesians*, 18.

18   Howard Kee points out that the aim of the magical formulas used in the Greek magical papyri is largely to protect from demons (*Medicine, Miracle and Magic in New Testament Times*, SNTSMS, vol. 55 [Cambridge, England: Cambridge University Press, 1986], 111-112).

importance for our subject. Mark inserts the encounter with the devil at the beginning of Jesus' ministry and at the beginning of the Gospel itself. It follows Jesus' baptism and the declaration of divine approval, which also provides a clue to Jesus' mission, i.e., to act as God's representative. Satan is present but his influence is inconsequential: there is no dialog, and no details are given except that Satan tempted Jesus.

By giving such a minor role to the devil and by portraying Jesus as completely in control, Mark provides a portrait of Satan which, far from being the all-powerful entity that many believed him to be, actually reduces him to an insignificant actor in the presence of Jesus. Like a fly in the house, Satan is annoying but of no real consequence. The text emphasizes the power of Jesus and the irrelevance of Satan.

Let's not forget that Mark was targeting an audience who believed in and was terrorized by the powers of the demonic world. An important part of Mark's agenda was to demystify and "declaw" the devil. The little attention Mark awards him in this passage would certainly contribute to that. If Jesus was so powerful that even Satan was no threat whatsoever, then demons would pose even less of a threat. This is exactly what we should expect to see in Mark's subsequent reports of demonic encounters.

Mark 1: 21-28: *They went to Capernaum; and when the sabbath came, he entered the synagogue and taught. They were astounded at his teaching, for he taught them as one having authority, and not as the scribes. Just then there was in their synagogue a man with an unclean spirit, and he cried out, "What have you to do with us, Jesus of Nazareth? Have you come to destroy us? I know who you are, the Holy One of God." But Jesus rebuked him, saying, "Be silent, and come out of him!" And the unclean spirit, convulsing him and crying with a loud voice, came out of him. They were all amazed, and they kept on asking one another, "What is this? A new teaching—with authority! He commands even the unclean spirits, and they obey him." At once his fame began to spread throughout the surrounding region of Galilee.*

In this passage, Jesus encounters a man possessed by an evil spirit. The spirit recognizes who Jesus really is and acknowledges Jesus' power to destroy him. Jesus exorcizes the man by commanding the spirit to be silent and to come out. Note that Jesus did not need to perform any special ritual or utter magical formulas: The spirit is unceremoniously dismissed and immediately leaves. The witnesses recognize Jesus' exceptional authority: The Son of God commands and the evil spirits obey. This passage confirms Jesus' absolute authority over demons in Jewish territory.

Mark 1:32-34: *That evening, at sundown, they brought to him all who were sick or possessed with demons. And the whole city was gathered around the door. And he cured many who were sick with various diseases, and cast out many demons; and he would not permit the demons to speak, because they knew him.*

Mark 1:32-34 reports that people brought the sick and the demon-possessed to Jesus and he "cast out many demons;…" He also had the authority to forbid them to reveal his real messianic identity. This event that occurred at Capernaum (Mark 1:21-28) demonstrates that Jesus' irresistible authority over demons was not an isolated incident or a fortunate coincidence. It worked every time.

Mark 3:11: *Whenever the unclean spirits saw him, they fell down before him and shouted, "You are the Son of God!"*

This passage removes all doubt as to Jesus' authority over evil spirits. Wherever they encounter him, they recognize his absolute authority, fall down in front of him and have no choice but to obey his orders.

Mark 3:14-15: *And he appointed twelve, whom he also named apostles, to be with him, and to be sent out to proclaim the message, and to have authority to cast out demons.*

Jesus' authority could be transferred to others at will. In 3:15, Jesus gives his apostles the authority to preach and also "to cast out demons." This text shows that the transfer of authority was a straightforward and effective procedure; there was no need for special rituals or magic formulas.

One other encounter found in chapter 5 is particularly significant.

Mark 5:1-20: *They came to the other side of the sea, to the country of the Gerasenes. And when he had stepped out of the boat, immediately a man out of the tombs with an unclean spirit met him. He lived among the tombs; and no one could restrain him any more, even with a chain; for he had often* *been restrained with shackles and chains, but the chains he wrenched apart, and the shackles he broke in pieces; and no one had the strength to subdue him. Night and day among the tombs and on the mountains he was always howling and bruising himself with stones.*

When he saw Jesus from a distance, he ran and bowed down before him; and he shouted at the top of his voice, "What have you to do with me, Jesus, Son of the Most High God? I adjure you by God, do not torment me." For he had said to him, "Come out of the man, you unclean spirit!" Then Jesus asked him, "What is your name?" He replied, "My name is Legion; for we are many." He begged him earnestly not to send them out of the country. Now there on the hillside a great herd of swine was feeding; and the unclean spirits begged him, "Send us into the swine; let us enter them." So he gave them permission. And the unclean spirits came out and entered the swine; and the herd, numbering about two thousand, rushed down the steep bank into the sea, and were drowned in the sea.

The swineherds ran off and told it in the city and in the country. Then people came to see what it was that had happened. They came to Jesus and saw the demoniac sitting there, clothed and in his right mind, the very man who had had the legion; and they were afraid. Those who had seen what had happened to the demoniac and to the swine reported it. Then they began to beg Jesus to leave their neighborhood. As he was getting into the boat, the man who had been possessed by demons begged him that he might be with him. But Jesus refused, and said to him, "Go home to your friends, and tell them how much the Lord has done for you, and what mercy he has shown you." And he went away and began to proclaim in the Decapolis how much Jesus had done for him; and everyone was amazed.

There is some debate as to the exact location of the "country of the Gerasenes," but it's not a significant issue for our purposes. What is important to note is that Jesus enters pagan territory. It was commonly believed in the ancient world that gods ruled over specific regions. That principle would limit a god's power and authority over his appointed territory. By this point in Mark's story, we know that Jesus has absolute authority over demons in Jewish territory. We can assume that his ability to control these demons derives from Yahweh. That leads us to the million-dollar question: Would Jesus' authority extend to Gentile territory where, in principle, he would not have access to God's power? This text was written partly to answer this question since it would naturally occur to the original readers.

Mark 5:2-5 describes the man's condition in great detail. The only piece of information we are not given is how he ended up in this situation. Mark is primarily concerned about showing the outcome of an encounter between Jesus and this extreme case of demon possession.

Mark creates a sense of urgency right from the outset: this creature from hell confronts Jesus as soon as he lands on the shore. The allusion to the man coming out of the tombs should not surprise us. This is where demons were expected to be. But ancient readers may have expected this to pose a problem for Jesus since cemeteries were considered to be unclean places and may therefore have weakened his ability to intervene.

Three forms of alienation are mentioned:
- This man is alienated from human society: he is banished and often in restraints.
- He is alienated from his family: he lives in tombs.
- He is alienated from himself: he is completely out of control.

Not only is this man beyond human restraint, he has very little control over his own self. He is self-destructive and clearly does not enjoy his condition. He is not like a vampire who considers his need for human blood a happy compromise for the promise of immortality. No! This man is consumed by anguish and pain. Sometimes, the agony is so intense, all he can do is scream. If we could only hear and see, it would freeze our blood. There is very little humanity left in this man who has degenerated into an animal. This is undoubtedly the worst case of demon possession one could imagine.

Mark chooses to report this worst case scenario because it shows the extent of destruction evil can do in a person's life. Can such a man be redeemed? Will Jesus' power be effective in this foreign and unclean place? This man's case is not unique. Evil always produces destruction in those who are exposed to it. Such cases of human misery can be seen every night in the streets of every major North American city.

In verse 6, something remarkable and unexpected happens to this man. In spite of what evil has done to him, in spite of whatever personal choices land him in this mess, in spite of his lost humanity, and in spite of his degenerative condition, something truly amazing happens. Three verbs underline an extraordinary chain of events:

1. The demon-possessed man *sees* Jesus.
In his condition, one would not expect this man to see much. And yet, as soon as Jesus enters his territory, he sees him.
2. He *runs* to Jesus.
3. He *falls* on his knees.

Mark reveals something extremely important about human nature and the real power of demons. Regardless of their condition, regardless of what evil has done to them, men and women always retain some spark of humanity. They always maintain the ability to turn to Jesus Christ. Nothing can eliminate this innate human capability. While God has an infinite capacity and willingness to extend his reach into the deepest recesses of the human soul, every man and woman has the ability to reach out to God, even when all hope seems lost.

In verses 7-8, we note the complete absence of struggle and resistance on the part of the demons. At the mere sight of Jesus, the demons surrender. In fact, they beg for the best terms of capitulation possible, nothing else. Their goose is cooked, and they know it.

The fact that Jesus asks the demon his name in verse 9 does not indicate Jesus is having difficulty subduing the demons. The question and its answer are inserted into the narrative to demonstrate the degree of demonic influence this man is under. "Legion," the man answers. Mark uses this expression to show that whatever possessed this man was anything but trivial. A literal reading of the Roman military term "legion" suggests that the man was inhabited by 4000-6000 demons. Here is where it gets interesting and extremely relevant for our discussion. Those who think that demons are extraordinarily powerful beings need to think again. A full contingent of demons, even as many as six thousand of them, could not keep this man from seeking help from Jesus Christ.

The pig episode reported in verses 11-13 is bizarre to say the least. Couldn't Jesus have chased these demons into thin air? Of course, he could have. But then, how could anyone be sure that Jesus actually chased that legion of demons? It was crucial that the demons be allowed to go into the pigs to demonstrate that this man was actually delivered from these demons, and to establish without a shadow of a doubt that Jesus had absolute authority over demons, "domestic" or "foreign"!

While this text confirms the existence of evil and disembodied spirits, it also shows that the range of freedom they enjoy is severely limited. They cannot keep the man from interacting with Jesus. They need Jesus' permission to invade a herd of pigs. And when Jesus gives them the green light, even with a ratio of three to one (6000 demons to 2000 pigs!), they appear to experience major difficulties with the pigs. I have no way to be sure, but I think Mark is making a little joke at the demons' expense. It is interesting to note that once they enter into the pigs, the herd instantaneously runs into the sea and drowns. While I don't want to read too much into the text, it certainly appears that the demons were powerless to keep those pigs from panicking in the face of this sudden invasion and rushing in terror towards their own destruction.

The authority of Jesus over demons and their impotence are further demonstrated by the depiction, in verses 14-17, of a man who is now back in control. He is dressed, sitting down and is mentally back in the saddle. Verses 18-20 portray the man as completely healed. Jesus entreats him to go back to his community and to tell others what happened. This man who had been reduced to the level of an animal, bent on his self-destruction, cut off from human contact and without hope, is now redeemed. He has even found a new reason to live.

After chapter 9, Mark reports no further encounters with demons. It's as though he is saying that enough has been said. There were more important things to deal with. If a reader still had doubts about the real nature of demons after reading the first nine chapters, that person needed to go back to square one.

Meat Sacrificed to Idols (1 Corinthians 8, 10)

At some point in his early missionary career, the apostle Paul brought the gospel to the city of Corinth. Many people accepted Paul's message and a Christian community was born. As was typical for the times, many Corinthians held a strong belief in demons and magic. As new Christians, they had a problem. Much of the meat sold in markets or available at social events originated from animals that had been sacrificed to pagan deities.[19] It was possible to obtain meat that had not been sacrificed to idols, but it

---

19 See F. F. Bruce, *I & II Corinthians*, The New Century Bible Commentary (Grand Rapids, MI: Eerdmans, 1971), 78.

was much less available and therefore much more costly. Uncertain about what to do, the Corinthian believers requested some guidance from Paul. The issue was not simply that this meat had been sacrificed to idols. The idols themselves were really nothing, since the Roman deities did not actually exist (1 Cor. 8:1-8). But, as Paul clarifies, although there is no such thing as an idol, demons are real:

> Consider the people of Israel; are not those who eat the sacrifices partners in the altar? What do I imply then? That food sacrificed to idols is anything, or that an idol is anything? No, I imply that what pagans sacrifice, they sacrifice to demons and not to God. I do not want you to be partners with demons (1 Cor. 10:18-20).

Here we have a problem that commentators do not generally appreciate to its full value. If, as Paul observes, these sacrifices were offered to demons; and if, as the Gentiles believed, demons could by some magic take control of people without their consent;[20] then eating meat sacrificed to idols/demons should have represented a major issue for Paul. In the perspective of that worldview, sacrificing meat to an idol—i.e., a demon—implied that the meat would become contaminated by that demon. Eating such meat would theoretically enable the demon to transfer to the person, thus resulting in demon-possession.[21] This is what is meant by a "magical" model of demon infection.

This understanding of demon contamination is in line with what most demonic warfare writers teach today. It is generally believed that any contact with objects, places, activities or people related in any way to the demonic or the occult will most likely put the person in a vulnerable position. The mode of infection is oddly similar to catching the flu. The odds of contracting a flu bug proportionately increase as one is exposed to people or objects that may have come into contact with infected people. Transposed on the spiritual plane, if a young boy plays a video game that

---

20   According to G. J. Riley, "Demons could not only attack but also indwell humans and cause many types of ills… They [demons] could be exorcised by providing a substitute host body, usually an animal, but also a figurine or even a reed of the same size as the human sufferer" (See "Demon," in *Dictionary of Deities and Demons* in the Bible, ed.. Karel van der Toorn, Bob Becking, and Pieter W. van der Horst [Grand Rapids, MI: Eerdmens, 1999], 237.

21   H. Conzelmann writes, "Sacrifices would make the demons into gods, powers, and bring the participants into bondage to them" (1 *Corinthians*, Hermeneia [Philadelphia, PA: Fortress Press], 173).

uses demonic themes, that boy exposes himself to "catching" a demon or two. Following the same logic, if a person associates with those who participate in role-playing games (such as *Dungeons and Dragons*) or other occult-related activities, that person will most likely "catch" a demon. A couple who buys a house that belonged to a Satanist is in serious risk of being oppressed or possessed by demons.

If this is how individuals become infected by demons, then these scenarios must be taken seriously and every effort must be made to avoid any contact whatsoever with objects or places infected by demons. Christians need to do a thorough audit of everything they own, the house they live in and the place they work to forestall any possibility of demonic infection. Along the same line of thought, Christians should take every imaginable precaution to ensure their children are never exposed to any item, person or activity that might have any association with the occult. Everyone should perform an ancestry audit to verify that no doors were ever opened for demons to enter the family line. Children should never be allowed to participate in a field trip to the local Buddhist temple; demons lurk there too and could surreptitiously take possession of them.

It goes without saying, then, that if we don't know how to perform the kind of spiritual audits these scenarios entail, we must enlist the help of a spiritual consultant to tell us you which of our personal possessions represent a problem and to perform the rituals that will exorcise infected locations. If we don't, so this theory goes, we expose ourselves to co-habiting with demons and to the possibility of being infected. This may sound farfetched, but some demonic warfare proponents (and other Christians) promote the necessity of retaining a spiritual specialist to exorcise a home before actually taking possession of it.[22]

Interestingly, house contractors who sell to Asian immigrants regularly hire a *Fengshui* consultant who performs community blessing rituals to help ensure the future resident's prosperity and happiness. These consultants also provide detailed instructions regarding the architectural specifications of the homes: No doors to the north so that evil spirits will not enter; and staircases must end at a right angle to the door so that vital energy is not

---

22 This website provides a typical description of the practice:
http://www.exorcisms.co.uk/exorcismintroduction.htm (accessed October 1, 2007).

lost through the front door. Sometimes chicken blood is even sprinkled on the building site to expel demons.

If Paul had held to this kind of belief, he would have warned his readers very explicitly about the danger that meat infected by demons represented. Surely, he would have said something like: "Stay away from such meat, because it has been infected by demons. If you consume this meat, the demons will in turn contaminate you." He would have vehemently exhorted his people to stay away from such meat in order to avoid demonic transference.

Instead, how does Paul respond?

First, the apostle makes the astonishing recommendation that the Corinthian Christians should feel free to buy anything sold in the meat market: "*Eat whatever is sold in the meat market without raising any question on the ground of conscience*" (1 Cor. 10:25). The same advice went to a Christian invited to eat dinner. "*If an unbeliever invites you to a meal and you are disposed to go, eat whatever is set before you without raising any question on the ground of conscience.*" (1 Cor. 10:27). No conditions. No ifs, buts or maybes. His advice is clear and to the point.

The apostle's response is very significant for us. As far as the meat is concerned, Paul has no worries whatsoever. He rejects the suggestion that meat sacrificed to idols may have quasi-magical powers. He is not concerned that meat might be instrumental in bringing about demon possession in any way or shape. A piece of meat is a piece of meat! No more, no less!

Paul is very clear about this issue. But how does he know? On what basis can he so categorically declare there is no harm whatsoever in consuming meat sacrificed to idols or demons when, intuitively, most of us would probably adopt a much more cautious approach? Let us look at two texts that will shed some light on this question: 1 Corinthians 8:4-7 and 10:25-26.

In 8:4-7, Paul settles the issue of idols. Idols are nothing, because there are no other deities than God the Father.

Hence, as to the eating of food offered to idols, we know that "no idol in the world really exists," and that "there is no God but one." Indeed, even though there may be so-called gods in heaven or on earth—as in fact there are many gods and many lords—yet for us there is one God, the Father, from whom are all things and for whom we exist, and one Lord, Jesus Christ, through whom are all things and through whom we exist. It is not everyone, however, who has this knowledge. Since some have become so accustomed to idols until now, they still think of the food they eat as food offered to an idol; and their conscience, being weak, is defiled.

In this passage, Paul essentially reflects the monotheistic view of God that characterizes the Old Testament. An idol is nothing because the existence of other gods is simply incompatible with the Old Testament belief that there is only one God: i.e., Yahweh.

In 10:26, Paul provides a definitive answer to the meat issue by quoting Psalm 24:1: "*The earth is the Lord's, and everything in it*" (NIV).

As it turns out, Paul's answer is ridiculously simple. The apostle does not work from some mysterious or esoteric revelation from God. The source of Paul's certainty comes from his theological starting point or, if one prefers, the basic set of assumptions he brings to the controversy. In these texts, Paul gives an insight into the core of his theological framework: creation theology.

The argument is surprisingly straightforward. In 8:4-7, Paul states there is only one God. As we saw in the previous chapter, this same declaration in ancient Israel signaled the end of magic. Since the effectiveness of magical powers depended on divine action, eliminating the gods necessarily eliminated the cosmic architecture needed to support the magical sphere. By extension, Paul's statement effectively eliminates the structure that would enable the type of demonic transfer pagans believed would occur between the infected meat and the consumer.

The second proposition found in 10:26 alludes to the intrinsic goodness of the physical universe. Simply stated, Paul declares that a piece of wood is a piece of wood or, to be more precise, a piece of meat is a piece of meat.

So, to answer some of the questions I am often asked: Can people become demon-possessed simply because of an object they have, a place they have visited, or suspicious people they have had contact with? Do I need to hire a spiritual warfare specialist to exorcise my new house? If we take Paul's assertions seriously, I would answer all these questions with a resounding no! These fears are based on superstitious pagan beliefs that fly in the face of the Judeo-Christian view of the universe. People cannot become demon-possessed because of an accidental association with a suspicious object or a place. There is no basis to suggest that houses can somehow be demonized. Although Christians may derive some comfort from exorcising a house, there is no reason whatsoever to believe that such rituals have any bearing on spiritual reality.

On the other hand, Paul does not suggest that idol worship is inconsequential and should be taken lightly. There is indeed a very serious problem with offering sacrifices to idols/demons. But the difficulty is not in the sphere of the magical or occult. The real issue behind idol worship is in the realm of the ethical. Paul points out two distinct problems linked to eating meat sacrificed to idols. First of all, the issue of loyalty and conscience: *"You cannot drink the cup of the Lord and the cup of demons. You cannot partake of the table of the Lord and the table of demons"* (1 Cor. 10:21). Paul reasserts that we cannot indiscriminately participate in activities that blatantly contradict the Christian faith. Our allegiance to Jesus-Christ has real implications for the way we live, work and play. Paul's words echo what Jesus meant when he said that *"you cannot serve God and wealth"* (Matt 6:24). Either we give allegiance to one or we serve the other.

The second caveat that Paul introduces into the discussion concerns the matter of community. The issue is underlined in 1 Corinthians 10:28-33:

> But if someone says to you, "This has been offered in sacrifice," then do not eat it, out of consideration for the one who informed you, and for the sake of conscience—I mean the other's conscience, not your own. For why should my liberty be subject to the judgment of someone else's conscience? If I partake with thankfulness, why should I be denounced because of that for which I give thanks? So, whether you eat or drink, or whatever you do, do everything for the glory of God. Give no offense to Jews or to Greeks or to the church of God, just as I try to please everyone in everything I do, not seeking my own advantage, but that of many, so that they may be saved.

In this text, Paul asserts that it may in fact be appropriate to refrain from eating meat sacrificed to idols; not because there is something intrinsically wrong with the meat, but for the sake of those whose conscience could be offended by that action. There are people whose conscience is too weak to understand the freedom of others. For Paul, it is not acceptable to exercise one's freedom if it results in the loss of someone else's faith.

It is imperative to understand Paul's argument correctly. The apostle does state that there is no issue with sacrificial meat in and of itself. Whether such meat has been exposed to demons is completely irrelevant. There is no danger of accidentally catching an evil spirit simply by eating such meat. Paul addresses the issue of the meat sacrificed to idols/demons at face value. There is no attempt whatsoever to discern a deeper, magical or occult sublayer of reality. The issue is simply defined in terms of ethics/allegiance/conscience and resolved in the realm of reason and compassion. Just as in the Gospel of Mark, this text gives no inkling at all of any reality to an occult understanding of demonic influence.

Paul's theological framework allows absolutely no reason to harbor and nurture fear, whether it be the fear of places, things, people, computer games, amulets, etc. Here is one concrete example of what that means: I personally have no fear at all of voodoo curses. Frankly, even if a sorcerer put a curse on me, I would not even pray for God's protection. Why? Because there is no basis to attribute any reality to such curses; they are just words. These words may impress a Haitian villager; they may cause an illness or perhaps even a death, but only because the villager believes in the power of these words. In that context, the worldview or a plausibility structure supports the curse and makes it effective. I will not deny that uttering a curse against a person may have an extremely negative impact on that individual. But I maintain that if it is the case, it is not because the curse has any intrinsic power. The potential effectiveness of the curse lies in the powerful belief system of the victim. In addition, if the person has given allegiance to demonic spirits, the effect would be that much more effective. I have no fear of occult objects; they are just things. I have no fear of attending a New Age convention. I may need wisdom to relate my faith, and I may indeed need to ask God's Spirit for the ability to speak to the hearts of these nature worshipers, but I don't need to pray for some quasi-magical, make-believe bubble of spiritual protection. Yes, there might be some danger associated with these things. But if we take Paul seriously, then we must admit and believe that the threat is not in the realm of the magical.

Conclusions
Demons Are for Real!

Mark and the apostle Paul both take for granted that demonic beings really exist. The Gospel of Mark does not present Jesus as someone who merely accommodated the naive beliefs of the superstitious people around him. Jesus recognizes the reality of Satan and demons: he addressed them directly, and he dismissed them. In Mark, the demons are real entities. Some form of manifestation such as illness, healing or screaming often accompanies their presence and departure. Outward demonic manifestations are emphasized, particularly when it is critical to demonstrate the power of Jesus Christ, such as in the case of the demon-possessed man whose demons enter into a herd of pigs (Mark 5:13).

In 1 Corinthians, Paul carefully distinguishes between idols and demons. The first have no objective existence—an assessment essentially derived from Creation theology (1 Cor. 8:4-6). But if there are no idols, Paul does, however, clearly state that demons exist: "*Consider the people of Israel; are not those who eat the sacrifices partners in the altar? What do I imply then? That food sacrificed to idols is anything, or that an idol is anything? No, I imply that what pagans sacrifice, they sacrifice to demons and not to God. I do not want you to be partners with demons*" (1 Corinthians 10:18-20).

Demonic Influences and Human Illness

In contrast to what we often hear from the demonic warfare crowd, there is no biblical basis to propose a direct cause and effect relationship between demonic influence and human illness. In 1 Corinthians, Paul moves away from that kind of understanding by pointing out that there is absolutely no intrinsic harm in consuming meats that were exposed to demons. Meat, even meat offered to demons, is only meat!

There are many instances in Mark's Gospel where illness is differentiated from demon possession.[23] Evidently, Jesus and his audience had the ability to distinguish between one and the other. How they did so is not clear; this is an issue I will address more explicitly later on. For now, it is sufficient to point out that there are no grounds to accept that all human ailments result from demonic activity. The belief that illnesses, particularly afflictions of a psychological character, are always the by-product of demonic influence attributes much more power to demonic beings than is warranted. It negates sin and the messy complexity of the human condition. It invalidates the notion of human responsibility.

All manner of human foibles have been attributed to some kind of demonic activity. There are ostensibly demons of gluttony, demons of

---

23 See Mark 1:32-34, 1:40-41; 2:1-12; 3:1-6; 5:21-24, 35-43; 5:25-34; 7:31-37; 8:22-25; 10:46-52.

lust, demons of anger, laziness, shyness, depression, etc., etc. In fact, there seem to be as many demons as there are human vices and weaknesses. This tendency to attribute every negative human emotion to demons can be very dangerous, particularly for people who are at a vulnerable stage of their lives. Teenagers, for example, typically find themselves in the throes of dramatic physical and hormonal changes. To teach a fourteen-year old boy that his sudden and sometimes overwhelming interest in girls is the result of demonic oppression may be much more psychologically and socially destructive than simply teaching him that this is a normal biological development. It is much healthier for a person to recognize the difficult realities of human life and to deal with them responsibly than to engage in futile demonic searches which, in extreme cases, may even trigger clinical depression or some other form of psychological disorder in people who may be predisposed.

The Power of Demons

In contrast to what 1st century men and women believed about the overwhelming and stealth-like powers of demons, Paul and Mark present a surprisingly subdued portrait of these creatures.

In 1 Corinthians, Paul forcefully undermines the belief in a magical/occult relationship between demonic spirits and people. Contrary to expectations, he sees no inherent threat whatsoever in eating meats used in idol/demon worship. *"Eat whatever is sold in the meat market without raising any question….,"* he writes. There were ethical issues involved in the consumption of such meat, but Paul insists there is nothing intrinsically dangerous about meat sacrificed to idols. At least two things are evident in Paul's writings: 1) demons do not have the kind of power pagans assumed they had; 2) Paul suggests a reconfiguration of the relationship between demonic powers and human beings, one based on reason rather of magic.

The Gospel of Mark portrays Satan as a nuisance, not as the all-powerful being he was often believed to be. Demons, for their part, are shown to be powerless in the presence of Jesus Christ. They are more like flies to be shooed away than overwhelming ork-like creatures that fiercely feed on the souls of helpless men. This characterization of Satan and demons is extremely important to note. Most often, people then and now, have had the propensity to attribute enormous powers to these beings. In terms of the way Mark depicts demons in his gospel, it is more correct to think of demons as empty shadows than to cultivate the images of powerful angels of darkness we too often see on Hollywood screens.

Essentially, Mark is attempting to communicate that demons are not the superhuman beings his contemporaries believed them to be, and that their powers ultimately derive from our own belief system. Far from being dark and powerful monsters that can irresistibly crush human souls with their fingers—as we are always tempted to believe—they are actually pathetic clowns, shadows and vapor mists that suddenly evaporate like dew in sunlight.

Demons are real, but their reality is mere illusion in the presence of the massive absoluteness of God. And if we think about it carefully, how could it be otherwise?

Whatever else demonic beings might be, they are by definition separated from God. Real power and substance are only found in God. Outside of him, there is only shadow, darkness, the mere whisper of reality. The only power these entities can possibly have is the power humans mistakenly and naively attribute to them. Mark vigorously debunks one of the great lies his contemporaries had bought into and that many even today still believe: Those demons have a power that is virtually irresistible. According to Mark, nothing could be further from the truth.

Demonic beings derive their power, not from themselves, but from the men and women upon whom they prey. The power of demons ultimately hinges on the belief system of the cultures in which they navigate.

This is the only possible explanation to account for the frequency and intensity of demonic manifestations in certain cultures. The reason demonic manifestations are so prevalent in Africa, Haiti or India and relatively scarce in the Western world is linked to a worldview that cultivates belief in demons in the former but generally ignores their existence in the latter. This is not to say that demons are not active on North American soil. What I am suggesting is that demonic manifestations such as overt demon-possession are not nearly as frequent in America because a large portion of the population holds to a belief system that does not naturally incorporate the reality of demons or the necessity to get actively involved with such creatures. On the other hand, we cannot deny the existence in America of subcultures where belief in and involvement with demons are actively promoted. For instance, we are more likely to observe a higher number of demonic manifestations amongst Louisiana Voodooists or California Satanists than in Nebraska.

A good example of the power of belief is the first impression our dog may leave on a guest. The dog we own is a gentle 14-year-old mixed Shitzu/Lhasa Apso. Though the dog is perfectly inoffensive, it does have a relatively loud, German Shepherd-like bark that roars into life whenever someone rings the bell. At first, the guest is certain there is a ferocious 150-pound dog barreling down the hallway. That false impression is quickly dispelled when the harmless mutt actually appears. The only way a man could possibly be intimidated is if he kept his back turned to the dog.

It is the same with demons. They can only terrorize those who give them the power to terrorize. In that respect, animists and most demonic warfare specialists commit the same error: they inadvertently empower demons by maintaining a belief system that attributes great power to them.

Demonic Harm

One could conclude from my writing so far that demons are inoffensive beings, annoying perhaps, but essentially harmless. That would not be accurate. In fact, demons can indeed inflict severe damage to human beings. The case of the demon-possessed man in Mark 5 is an unmitigated example of the harm demons can do to a person. Some might even conclude from this and other examples in the Gospels that there is some merit to the belief that demons are powerful stealth-like creatures. It is important, when considering these difficult questions, to exercise great care not to buy into ideas that essentially reflect a pagan worldview. As we observed earlier, when we deal with the supernatural, it is relatively easy to embrace beliefs that do not reflect the biblical worldview.

We must also beware of the risk of arriving at definitive and sweeping conclusions from silence. Mark 5 and similar Gospel texts could mislead us to conclude that demons are indeed ominous creatures, and that they do possess the ability to infect human beings without their consent or their knowledge. But it's not quite that simple. For one, though the condition of the man in the Mark 5 narrative is clearly linked to demonic influence, Mark does not explain how the demon-possessed man—or, for that matter, any of the other people mentioned in his Gospel—ends up in the unfortunate condition in which he finds himself. In fact, Mark 5 and other demon-casting texts offer little, if anything at all, about the causes behind the demonic infection or the process that led these people to that state. It's not the purpose of the narratives. So then to conclude from these reports that demons can infect human beings through some kind of unconscious magical or supernatural process is to venture beyond what the texts actually say.

Whether demons can affect human beings is not the issue. The question that needs clarifying relates to the mode of interaction between the demonic and human spheres. Mark clearly shows that demons are and can be dangerous. The issue is to define as precisely as possible the exact nature of the threat they represent, and how that threat materializes itself in the lives of men and women.

Chapter 4:

Practical Issues in Demonic Warfare

The most obvious difference between the demonic warfare model generally adopted today and the one I propose focuses on the manner in which demons interact with human beings. Based on Genesis 1-3, I contend that our environment is not governed in any way, shape or form by magical forces. Demonic beings, though real, have no effective control over the physical universe and have very limited intrinsic power. Whatever influence they may have is derived either from the worldview of the culture in which they are present or from human agency.

Undoubtedly, the main reason behind the broad acceptance of the Third Wave movement's demonic ideology is the perception that it provides practical solutions to a variety of real-life challenges. These range from our inability to reach a city for Jesus Christ to successfully liberating a demon-possessed person.

In this section, I intend to draw out the implications of this study for a number of practical issues that face pastors, church leaders and lay people in their respective ministries. The material addresses five of the most commonly asked questions I have received over the years. The intent is not so much to comprehensively answer all these questions, but to spell out the basic implications of the framework I have developed throughout these pages.

FIVE QUESTIONS

Question #1: What is spiritual warfare?

The first question deals with the exact nature of spiritual warfare. This section argues for the importance of distinguishing between the broader spiritual struggle all Christians face as they seek to remain faithful to their calling as disciples and the more specific problem of how Christians deal with the demonic.

Question #2: Where does radical evil come from?

The second section briefly explores the broader question of evil and how it might relate to demonic influence.

Question #3: Why does demon-possession seem to be that much more prevalent in non-Western or animistic cultures?

This question addresses the apparent divergence in overt demonic manifestations between Western and non-Western cultures.

Question #4: What should Christians do if they think they have encountered a person who appears to be demon-possessed?
The fourth section offers some practical guidelines dealing with people who appear to be demon-possessed.

Question #5: What about Ancestral Curses?
The final section addresses the question of whether the sins of our ancestors can, as many spiritual warfare specialists suggest, unwittingly open doors through which demons can affect generations of people up to the present.

Question #1: What is Spiritual Warfare?

Demonic warfare versus spiritual warfare
In this book, I have tended to use the expression "demonic warfare" rather than "spiritual warfare" in order to focus as narrowly as possible on what has proven to be the most controversial aspect of the recent spiritual warfare movement: i.e., the precise nature of the interaction between the demonic and human spheres. I chose this approach because I believe it is imperative that Christians address the issues that have become more and more prevalent in the Western world since the rise of the New Age movement and the increasing acceptance of the worldviews associated with eastern religions. I have also intentionally outlined a theoretical model that can be an effective framework for missionaries who are confronted with various expressions of spiritualism and, at times, extreme forms of demonic manifestations in the region of the world that is now commonly known as the "10/40 window."

I chose the term "demonic warfare" to indicate a distinction between that narrower sphere of inquiry and the broader concept of spiritual warfare. I consistently said there is no biblical basis for adopting a worldview that promotes fear of demons and belief in magic or occult powers. This is not to suggest, however, that there is no such a thing as a spiritual war, or that the Christian life is devoid of struggles. Such a view would not reflect how the Bible characterizes the Christian life.

For our struggle is not against enemies of blood and flesh...

Christians do indeed participate in a spiritual battle. Paul most explicitly alludes to it in Ephesians 6:12: *"For our struggle is not against enemies of blood and flesh, but against the rulers, against the authorities, against the cosmic powers of this present darkness, against the spiritual forces of evil in the heavenly places."* That Christians are involved in a spiritual struggle is not the issue. The real question concerns the precise nature of the struggle Paul refers to.

The Ephesians 6 passage is most commonly understood to denote the type of demonic warfare that Frank Peretti popularized in his novels, or that the more recent *Left Behind* series portrayed as Christians battle forces of darkness in a post-rapture world. Yet the fact that Paul is not suggesting some type of mysterious demonic warfare is made clear both by the broad categories he uses to denote the "enemy" forces and by the strategy he proposes. First, Paul observes that the spiritual struggle Christians are involved in has nothing to do with actual military action: "...our struggle is not against enemies of flesh and blood," he writes. The most immediate threat is not physical. Second, the allusion to the "rulers," the "authorities," "the cosmic powers of this present darkness," and the "spiritual forces of evil in the heavenly realms" underlines that the world's opposition to the Church is not to be identified with a particular person or institution. Rather, the world's hatred is universal, for the hearts of men and women are in a state of rebellion towards God (John 15:19). Paul wants to remind his readers of the grave spiritual threat that lurks around them.

What is the fundamental nature of this struggle? The metaphors Paul uses in 6:13-17 help clarify his meaning. Paul makes no allusion whatsoever to any kind of demon-casting exercise or magical ritual Christians should practice to ward off the powers of darkness. His exhortations are remarkably down to earth and underline a three-prong strategy that deals with attitudes, belief system and commitment to a biblical worldview.

Regarding attitudes, the apostle urges his readers to remain firm, steadfast and resolute: *"Put on the whole armor of God, so that you may be able to stand against the wiles of the devil"* (6:11). In other words, Paul encourages his readers to exemplify the qualities good soldiers must cultivate in order to defeat an enemy. He exhorts them not to be intimidated by the adversary.

The second part of Paul's three-prong strategy calls for his readers to draw strength from an appropriate set of beliefs. In typical military language, he calls them to be spiritually strong by putting on the full armor of God. Instead of appealing to magical incantations or practicing rituals, they are to clothe their minds and hearts with "the belt of truth" (v.14), to wield "the word of God" as a sword (v.17), to wear "as shoes" whatever will enable them to *proclaim* the gospel of peace (v.15).

Finally, Paul advocates an uncompromising commitment to these beliefs. The "shield of faith" (v.16) refers to the unswerving certitude that the truths found in God's Word are indeed authoritative and trustworthy. It is the "shield of faith" that extinguishes the missiles of the evil one, not magical rituals.

In The Realm of Reason! A Call to Spiritual Resilience!

The Ephesians 6 passage does not point to a form of mystical demonic warfare that plays itself out in a mysterious realm of action. The emphasis on resolve, truth, faith and constant prayer in verses 18 and 19 suggests a struggle in the realm of ideology/worldview and loyalty.

As we observed in Paul's treatment of meat sacrificed to idols/demons, the real question was not about whether the meat represented an occult danger to the Christians who consumed it. The real problem was ethical, and Paul resolved it in the realm of reason.

There are real dangers lurking for Christians. Paul's repeated appeals to pray underline that fact. But the threats lie in the realm of our allegiances, our convictions, our lifestyle, our choices; not in the realm of the occult and magic. In Paul's writings, spiritual warfare mostly denotes the tensions (theological, social, psychological), the conflicts, the ethical options and the worldview choices that Christians face daily. The spiritual warfare that Christians participate in ultimately plays itself out in the realm of reason. This observation is perfectly consistent with Paul's stress on the mind and his remarkable, even surprising, lack of attention to demonic warfare as such. Consider the following passages.

Therefore, since we are justified by faith, we have peace with God through our Lord Jesus Christ, through whom we have obtained access to this grace in which we stand; and we boast in our hope of sharing the glory of God" (Rom. 5:1-2).

I appeal to you therefore, brothers and sisters, by the mercies of God, to present your bodies as a living sacrifice, holy and acceptable to God, which is your spiritual worship. Do not be conformed to this world, but be transformed by the renewing of your minds, so that you may discern what is the will of God—what is good and acceptable and perfect (Rom. 12:1-2).

Finally, beloved, whatever is true, whatever is honorable, whatever is just, whatever is pure, whatever is pleasing, whatever is commendable, if there is any excellence and if there is anything worthy of praise, think about these things. Keep on doing the things that you have learned and received and heard and seen in me, and the God of peace will be with you (Phil. 4:8-9).

For in Christ Jesus neither circumcision nor uncircumcision counts for anything; the only thing that counts is faith working through love (Gal. 5:6).

Not only does Paul locate the real battle in the sphere of the mind and the will, but he also does not entertain the kind of irrational fear of and preoccupation with demonic powers that is so often observed in today's mainstream demonic warfare literature. On the contrary, Paul exudes a profound sense of peace and confidence, and he entreats the reader to seek the same.

Rejoice in the Lord always; again I will say, Rejoice. Let your gentleness be known to everyone. The Lord is near. Do not worry about anything, but in everything by prayer and supplication with thanksgiving let your requests be made known to God. And the peace of God, which surpasses all understanding, will guard your hearts and your minds in Christ Jesus (Phil. 4:4-7).

Paul expects the Christian life to be characterized by confidence, joy and peace. Not fear. Philippians 4:4-7 represents the entire tone of Paul's theology. His starting point is one of confidence in God. He does not fear the supernatural, as was common fare with pagans. Paul's writings include no exhortation to build mystical bubbles of protection; just sheer joy and confidence.

I could quote many other passages, but I think the point is clear. Paul constantly addresses himself to the intelligence of his readers. His exhortations always appeal to the will of the believer and encourage a deliberate choice to live for Jesus Christ.

Spiritual Warfare: One Metaphor amongst many

The use of the warfare metaphor as the predominant paradigm to describe the believer's life is to go beyond what the authors of Scripture intended, particularly when it comes to articulating the interaction between the human experience and the demonic world. Spiritual warfare is simply one of many metaphors Scripture uses to characterize different aspects of the Christian life.[1] Psalm 1 uses the metaphor of the tree to describe the life of the righteous. Paul exploits several images, such as: the sacrificial system to illustrate the importance of devotion to God (Rom. 12:1); the court of law to denote the idea of forgiveness and justification (Rom. 5:1); and the institution of slavery to express the notion of unconditional service to God (Rom. 6:17-18).

Each metaphor is certainly useful, but it also has inherent limitations. While the metaphor of spiritual warfare is helpful, it can lead to a grossly distorted perception of life if it is transformed into an overall principle of integration to characterize the Christian life.

To locate spiritual warfare in the realm of reason and our allegiances is completely consistent with Jesus' own approach. In Matthew 15:18-20, Jesus dismisses the idea that evil ultimately originates in the environment, whether it be from demons or various sociological factors. Instead, Jesus squarely identifies the human heart as the ultimate source of evil:

> *But what comes out of the mouth proceeds from the heart, and this is what defiles. For out of the heart come evil intentions, murder, adultery, fornication, theft, false witness, slander. These are what defile a person, but to eat with unwashed hands does not defile.*

---

1 In this respect, Sydney H. T. Page's survey of Satan and the demonic in the Bible is very helpful in presenting a balanced and hermeneutically sound study of demonic warfare. His analysis of Satan in apostolic teaching is particularly relevant (see *Powers of Evil*, 183-221).

Jesus' position is also completely consistent with what we find in the Old Testament where the ultimate responsibility for evil is never attributed to demonic beings. For example, the temptation narrative in Genesis 3 contains no reference to magic or occult powers lurking behind the scene. Besides the fact that the serpent could talk, he appears on the scene to deceive Eve with nothing but the power of persuasion. The serpent submits a straightforward question, and Eve has to choose her course of action based on her assessment of whether the serpent is telling the truth or not. It is important to note that Eve has all the elements at her disposal to arrive at a correct assessment of the serpent's statement. Eve's "conundrum" is not located in the realm of magic but in the realm of reason and allegiances.

In Genesis 4, Cain must choose whether to follow through on his desire to kill his brother Abel or to move away from the lethal yearning that is overwhelming him. The text identifies no outside agent involved in Cain's moral dilemma. In fact, God himself states that the decision is entirely within his purview:

> *The LORD said to Cain, "Why are you angry, and why has your countenance fallen? If you do well, will you not be accepted? And if you do not do well, sin is lurking at the door; its desire is for you, but you must master it (Gen. 4:6-7).*

The terrible conditions prevailing in Israel during the 8th century B.C. (see Amos, Hosea, Isaiah, Micah) further illustrate this point.[2] The root cause for the gross oppression—the exploitation of the poor and the vile idolatry that prevailed throughout the 8th century and for most of the kingship period—is never attributed to demonic forces. The prophets consistently hold the leaders responsible for Israel's sorry state and appeal to their reason, their conscience and their heart to change their course of action. The terrible conditions existing in the pre-exilic period are the outcome of the people's thirst for power and wealth, period! Never does

---

2   Rainer Albertz, in his authoritative treatment of the development of Israelite religion, provides an extremely insightful portrait of the social and religious situation that prevailed in 8th century B.C. Israel (see *A History of Israelite Religion in the Old Testament Period*, vol. 1, tr. by John Bowen [Louisville, KY: Westminster/John Knox Press, 1992], 156-186).

Scripture suggest that these conditions resulted from some territorial demonic spirit or other demonic oppression over Israel.

Conclusion: What is spiritual warfare?

In the New Testament, spiritual warfare mostly refers to the tensions, the conflicts, the ethical options and the worldview choices that Christians must face. These struggles are in the realm of reason and our allegiances, and believers cope with them with the supernatural help of the Holy Spirit (see John 7:38-39; 15:26; 16:15; Rom. 8:2-16; Eph. 2:18; 5:18, etc.).

Question #2: Where does radical evil come from?

In general, people are quite willing to accept that human beings themselves are the major cause of evil in this world. Some people's behavior may be exacerbated by the environment they grew up in, the abuse they suffered at the hands of others, or even the harsh conditions they live in. But when all is said and done, most people probably agree with Jesus' premise that evil ultimately takes shape in the human heart.

But for many of us, there are limits to how far we will take this idea. In extreme cases, the actions some people participate in are so vile and repulsive that some other explanation for this radical evil must be given. In order to give a concrete picture of what I mean by radical evil, let me relate two specific cases.

Putting a Face on Radical Evil: Paul Bernardo and Karla Homolka [3]

The first case involves what at first appears to be a dream couple. The young man, Paul Bernardo, was a seemingly well-to-do accountant. The young woman, Karla Homolka, was a pretty young woman hopelessly in love with Paul; she was willing to do literally anything to keep him by her side. Paul and Karla both come from middle-class families.

---

3   The detailed account of this story can be found in Stephen Williams' book, *Invisible Darkness: The Strange Case of Paul Bernardo and Karla Homolka* (New York, NY: Bantam, 1997). The summary provided here is inspired from the succinct description of the case by Marilyn Bardsley, Serial Killers: Partners in Crime, "Paul Bernardo and Karla Homolka," http://www.crimelibrary.com/serials/bernardo/bernmain.htm (accessed July 25, 2005)

Paul and Karla met in 1987 and were quite taken with each other. But there was a very dark side to their relationship. On one occasion, he asked her how she would feel about him if he were a rapist. Astonishingly, she indicated that it would be cool. So Paul, sometimes accompanied by Karla with a video camera, started raping women. By 1988, Paul had raped at least a dozen women.

Paul was always annoyed that Karla had not been a virgin when they first met. He strongly felt that it was her responsibility to provide him with access to her younger sister Tammy. Karla went along with the plan. Because she worked for a veterinarian, Karla was able to get some halothane, an anesthetic normally used on animals before surgery.

On December 23, 1990, they put their plan into effect and *both* raped Tammy. Unfortunately Tammy threw up and choked to death. The whole affair was captured on video for later reference. Paul and Karla phoned an ambulance, but led everyone to believe that Tammy had choked on her own vomit.

You'd think this horrible incident would have put the fear of God into the hearts of Paul and Karla. Not for one instant! Our couple from hell was just getting warmed up. Paul was pretty upset about losing Tammy and now wanted a replacement.

With Tammy dead, Karla desperately wanted to make it up to Paul. Karla knew a young teenager named Jane. One evening, she invited Jane to come to her house where Karla quickly managed to drug her. Once Jane was asleep, both Karla and Paul brutally raped her.

Later one night, while Paul was prowling a neighborhood looking for license plates to steal, he happened to meet a teenager who had been locked out of her house. He pulled a knife on Leslie, forced her into his car, and took his "catch" home. "While Karla slept, he began to videotape the fourteen-year-old Leslie naked and blindfolded. When Karla woke up, she was very angry that Paul had used their best champagne glasses to entertain his new toy. Finally, Karla came around and started being the obedient wife that Paul demanded."[4] On June 29, 1991, a husband and wife, canoeing on Lake Gibson, came upon a partially submerged block of concrete that contained the calf and the foot of a young woman. It was Leslie.

---

4   See Bardsley, "Paul Bernardo and Karla Homolka."

On November 30, 1991, 14-year old Terri Anderson was recruited to entertain the deadly couple. But after a while, she moved back to Youngstown, Ohio. Again, Paul and Karla needed a new toy. On April 16, 1992, Kristen French disappeared from a church parking lot. She had been abducted by the Bernardos. For a couple of days, they subjected this young woman to the worst of indignities, and then they killed her. A couple of weeks later, her naked, dismembered body was found in a ditch.

To make a long story short, Paul and Karla were eventually charged and convicted with the murder of all these girls.

Putting a Face on Radical Evil: Zosia
The second case is reported by Gregory Boyd in his book *God at War*. Historian Philip Friedman provides the following eyewitness account of what happened to a young Jewish girl living in the Warsaw ghetto during the Nazi occupation.

> Zosia was a little girl…the daughter of a physician. During an "action" one of the Germans became aware of her beautiful diamond-like dark eyes. "I could make two rings out of them," he said, "one for myself and one for my wife." His colleague is holding the girl. "Let's see whether they are really so beautiful. And better yet, let's examine them in our hands." Among the buddies exuberant gaiety breaks out. One of the wittiest proposes to take the eyes out. A shrill screaming and the noisy laughter of the soldier-pack. The screaming penetrates our brains, pierces our heart, the laughter hurts like the edge of a knife plunged into our body. The screaming and the laughter are growing, mingling and soaring to heaven. O God, whom will you hear first? What happens next is that the fainting child is lying on the floor. Instead of eyes two bloody wounds are staring. The mother, driven mad, is held by the women. This time they left Zosia to her mother. At one of the next "actions," little Zosia was taken away. It was, of course, necessary to annihilate the blind child. [5]

---

5 See Boyd, *God at War*, 33-34. The story reports an eyewitness account by historian Philip Friedman in P. Friedman, ed., *Martyrs and Fighters: The Epic of the Warsaw Ghetto* (New York, NY: Praeger, 1954), 166-167. Quoted in D. Rausch, *A Legacy of Hatred: Why Christians Must Not Forget the Holocaust* (Chicago, IL: Moody, 1984), 122.

These two cases are unimaginably evil. They represent what I consider to be perfect examples of radical evil. I personally lack words to express the depth of the horror I feel at such actions. Even describing these people's actions as satanic does not seem to do justice to what transpired there.

Where does such evil come from? Are some people innately evil? What kind of process can possibly lead a man or a woman to prey mercilessly on defenseless human beings?

Demonic Warfare Shrapnel

Some writers suggest that such horrific evil is impossible to imagine without the reality of some kind of cosmic warfare that spills over on the earth. People who commit such acts must be under some kind of demonic influence: controlled by demons of lust, demons of cruelty and demons of power. That might be true and maybe it is the best way to make sense of people like Paul and Karla. That's scary enough. But what is even scarier is *how* they might have fallen into such a state.

Demonic warfare writers propose a variety of methods by which people can be infected by the demonic. The following list is representative of what can be found in the literature:

- Participation in the occult
- Pornography
- Contact with an object or a place associated with an occult or pagan practice.
- Ancestral curses: A historical act of violence that opens a specific family line to demonic influence.
- Traumatic events: A person, particularly a child, becomes demon-possessed as a result of severe abuse or by witnessing an act of extreme violence.
- Exposure to violent video or computer games that have satanic overtones.

What I find particularly disconcerting about some of these possible mechanisms of demonic possession is their unpredictable character. The overall impression we get from such a list is that demonic oppression is akin to terrorism or catching a cold: It is virtually impossible to predict where it will come from or when it will strike. No one is safe and there is nowhere to hide. While one might argue that dabbling in the occult surely opens one up to demonic oppression, how can we possibly protect ourselves from an ancestral curse or from accidental contact with an occult object? It is as futile as trying to avoid catching cold viruses on an overcrowded bus. If this is truly how demons can possess people and transform them into the kind of monsters Paul Bernardo and Karla Homolka became, then we have to concede at the very least that we live in an extremely unpredictable universe where we always have to be on guard against the overwhelming powers of demonic beings who are capable of striking anytime and without warning.

As popular and widely held as this view might be, this understanding of the relationship between humans and demons is not consistent with the picture of the world as depicted in the Creation account. Nor does it agree with the reports of Jesus' encounters in the Gospel of Mark or with Paul's writings. There is no biblical justification for such a view. Let me make myself clear. I do not suggest at all that consumption of pornography and exposure to violent video games or the occult are harmless. These types of activities have profound repercussions both on the character of the people who indulge in them, and on the way they perceive themselves and their world. Addictions to pornography or video games are extremely harmful and often have far-reaching consequences. I do contend, however, that these activities—in and of themselves—do not necessarily or automatically open doors to demonic possession or oppression. I suspect that the mechanisms leading to demonization are much more complex and are ultimately entwined with human free will.

Still the fundamental question remains. If the Paul Bernardos and the Karla Homolkas of the world are not necessarily the product of overwhelming and stealthy demonic beings, what explanation can we possibly give to account for the existence of such wicked people? This is not an easy question. And frankly, while I think we are approaching the realm of mystery, let me nevertheless give a personal perspective on the issue.

First, a general statement. The Bible indicates that human beings are solicited by two voices: The voice that leads to God and the voice that leads away from God. A person who listens to the first will be ushered into an existence characterized by life. But the life of a person who listens to the voice that leads away from God will be characterized by death. This is the essence of God's command to Adam and Eve in Genesis 2:15-17 and the core of the Old Testament's entire wisdom tradition.[6] This idea is also expressed in various ways in the Gospel of John where those who believe in Jesus receive life but, those who reject him will experience death.[7]

The voice that leads to death originates from two sources. One of them is the human heart. The Genesis 3 account of the Fall teaches that something went terribly wrong with the human race. At some point in humanity's early history, something was broken in the deepest recesses of the human soul. Although no one can quite explain why this first act of disobedience had such catastrophic consequences on the human race, the reality is that this momentous event profoundly affected the entire course of human history. It is at this point that evil and suffering entered the world. While, as Genesis 3:22 suggests,[8] humanity discovered the true significance of free will and acquired a precious insight into moral and spiritual reality, the primordial choice also locked humanity into the sphere of death. Thus was ushered in the age of fear and misery, the age of superstition, idolatry and magic; the age of violence and war.

It is here, I believe, that we draw near the second and ultimate source of evil. While human nature was irremediably damaged by Adam and Eve's primordial act of disobedience, humans nevertheless retained a degree of freedom to choose between good or evil and the absolute ability to love or reject God. Moral evil emerges from this human free will: the unrestricted ability humans have to reject God and choose self, and the relative capability they have to make moral choices. In his classic treatment

---

6   For more details about the Old Testament wisdom tradition, I recommend Walter Brueggemann's very insightful treatment in *In Man We Trust* (Atlanta, GA: John Knox, 1972).

7   See, for example, John 3:15-18; 3:36; 5:24, 39-40; etc.

8   Gen. 3:22: "And the LORD God said, 'The man has now become like one of us, knowing good and evil. He must not be allowed to reach out his hand and take also from the tree of life and eat, and live forever.'"

of the problem of pain, C. S. Lewis writes:

I have tried to show in a previous chapter that the possibility of pain is inherent in the very existence of a world where souls can meet. When souls become wicked they will certainly use this possibility to hurt one another; and this, perhaps, accounts for four-fifths of the sufferings of men. It is men, not God, who have produced racks, whips, prisons, slavery, guns, bayonets, and bombs; it is by human avarice or human stupidity, not by the churlishness of nature, that we have poverty and overwork.[9]

I do not at all suggest, as did the great Jewish theologian Martin Buber,[10] that human beings face moral dilemmas from a neutral position. The account of the Fall and a number of Old and New Testament passages present a much more pessimistic view of human nature. One of the most unfortunate consequences of the Fall is that we are no longer morally neutral beings; human nature has now within itself the seeds of death and moral corruption. Not only do we seem to have a default position that causes us to lean away from God, we also have a potential for the worst kind of evil or cruelty imaginable.

The complexity of human spiritual reality is confirmed by the Cain and Abel story. While Cain gave in to his murderous impulse, God's intervention reminds us that Cain was not compelled to obey his impulse—he had a choice.

Paul confirms this in a number of passages.[11] And Jesus clearly alludes to this when he said:

But what comes out of the mouth proceeds from the heart, and this is what defiles. For out of the heart come evil intentions, murder, adultery, fornication, theft, false witness, slander. These are what defile a person, but to eat with unwashed hands does not defile. (Matt. 15:18-19).

---

9   C. S. Lewis, *The Problem of Pain* (New York, NY: HarperSanFrancisco, 2001 [1940]), 86.

10   See, for example, Martin Buber, *Good and Evil* (New York, NY: Scribners Sons, 1952).

11   See Rom. 1:18-32; 3:11-18; 3:21-26; 5:12; Eph. 2:1 (compare with Gen. 3:7; 3:8; 3:12; 4-11; 6:1-8; 6:11-13; Jer. 31:33; Matt. 15:17-20; John 3:16-21).

If we take Scripture at face value, then we have to conclude that no type of evil is beyond what we as human beings have the potential to commit. Men and women do not need any help from demons to engage in destruction and torture. In fact, Scripture always attributes primary responsibility to human beings for the evil they do. And, interestingly, accepting responsibility for our own actions is probably one of the most loathsome tasks we face. Just like our first parents, we innately tend to deflect responsibility from ourselves to someone or something else.

As horrendous as it may be, I believe that Paul Bernardo, Karla Homolka, or the Nazi soldiers who tortured and killed a defenseless little girl ultimately did what they did out of their own free will. No need to be possessed by demonic beings to do these things. In some respects, it would be comforting to think that we could only commit such acts of cruelty if we were to come under the influence of some hellish creature. To the woman who has been cheated on, the husband could say: "The devil made me do it." To the judge who presides over a murder, the perpetrator could say: "The devil made me do it." To the parents of a child who has been sexually abused, the pervert could say: "The devil made me do it." But that won't do! Scripture unambiguously teaches that we are responsible for our actions and we will be held accountable for them.

While evil forever springs anew from the depths of the human heart, evil needs a framework within which to be actualized. In that respect, our social environment represents the medium through which evil radiates. It constitutes the second source or, perhaps more accurately, the conduit for evil to expand into reality. Evil is not embodied through some mysterious process, as though it were an ominous cloud hanging over the earth. *Ideology is the mechanism through which evil is ultimately carried out.*

Consider the Jewish Holocaust: The idea of annihilating six million Jews did not just spontaneously emerge out of nowhere. The latent hatred for the Jews was already present in many parts of Europe. It found concrete expression in an ideology that taught the intrinsic superiority of the Aryan race and the necessity of eliminating any factor that could threaten the Third Reich's racial purity. The hatred was already there, but it was anti-Semitic propaganda and the Nazi machine that translated this nebulous hatred into the orgy of slaughter that became Nazi Germany's terrible legacy.

To further illustrate the mutual relationship between the human heart and the social environment, let me share a personal anecdote. As a French Canadian who grew up in Quebec, I used to hate those we called the "English." I was a pure-bred French Canadian whose people had been conquered by the "English" in 1759 and who, almost two hundred years later!!!, still carried a whole boat load of hatred for them. I had no concrete reason to hate the "English." I was not, in any objective sense, the victim of oppression. Quebec City had a reasonably good standard of living for the times; no worse— I am sure—and possibly better than places like Vermont or Kansas. I was free to speak French and to practice my religion. But I still hated the "English."

Why? First, the heart is a fertile ground for hatred—hatred comes fairly naturally to all of us. The potential for hatred that was already in me had been fertilized, nurtured and cultivated. There was an ideology of hatred that was circulated by relatives, teachers, friends and the media. Because the human heart has the potential to hate, the ideology of hatred found a ready and hospitable home in me, and in turn, found expression in my relationships with others. Incidentally, I turned away from that hatred when I committed my life to Jesus Christ. Only the love of Jesus Christ could smother the flames of hatred that consumed my soul.

So, where does that leave demons? Don't they play any role in human affairs? Assuming that demons exist, as Scripture asserts, how do they relate to us? By now, it should be perfectly clear to my readers that the relationship between the demonic and human spheres cannot be defined by occult or magical categories. There is no biblical foundation to believe that objects can transfer evil spirits or that there is any objective reality to occult and New Age powers. We simply don't catch demons the way we catch a cold.

Spiritual warfare, as the New Testament portrays it, is primarily defined in the realm of the rational and the moral. As disciples, Christians are called to live as godly people in a society whose values constantly clash with those of God's kingdom. This intrinsic opposition between the kingdom of God and the "world," to use the language of the apostle John, explains why Christians are involved in a spiritual war. By virtue of their allegiance to Christ and their presence in a world that is opposed to God, Christians must perpetually monitor themselves and readjust their course in respect to their allegiances, their lifestyle and their beliefs. It is those choices, taken daily and sometimes moment-by-moment, that eventually determine the quality of a person's life. Whether one is successful depends on the clarity of one's premises and the choices made in the face of life's challenges.

If purpose and clear premises determine one's ability to live for the kingdom, then it follows logically that any confusion in those areas can severely affect a person's ability to live for Christ. By definition, satanic activity seeks to oppose the work of God in the world.[12] When, for instance, Jesus called Peter "Satan" (Matt. 16:23), it wasn't that Peter had abruptly transformed into a vile demonic being. Peter was "satanic" in the sense that he, at that moment, opposed God's purpose. In the same sense, any action that opposes God's designs would be qualified as satanic.

It is essential to understand that demonic activity is perfectly satanic: It is bent on opposing God's purposes. If the quality of a person's discipleship depends on clear purpose and adequate premises, then demonic action must first and foremost be understood as that which most effectively promotes ideologies that confuse the mind of Christians and non-Christians alike.

Since God's purpose involves the creation of a new people—a redeemed people—then we can assume that demonic powers are actively working to keep human beings from accepting God's invitation to join that new people. The best tactic, if not the only one, is to call God's character and the nature of reality into question. This is exactly what the serpent did in the Garden of Eden. Nothing magical went on there. No occultism; no black magic at work. Only a simple question that challenged Eve to question God's character and whether he was really trustworthy. In effect, Eve and the serpent engaged in a life and death debate on what constitutes ultimate reality.

So, the question still remains: How do demons affect human beings? Based on what we have been able to ascertain regarding the ultimate nature of reality, I reiterate my conviction that demons have no supernatural powers they can bring to bear on individual human beings *to force them to act against their will*. I strongly suspect that demonic influence is mediated

---

12   The Hebrew word for Satan and its Greek equivalent both denote the one who opposes. Satan is the adversary

primarily through the social environment. Demonic forces likely piggyback on whatever is already active in our society to undermine God's credibility, to entice people away from God, and to promote destruction of life and God's purposes.

How exactly demons accomplish this today is not clear to me. Can demons actually manipulate our thinking? Can they supernaturally sow destructive thoughts in the minds of individual men and women? Based on the portrait of reality provided in Genesis 1-3, and contrary to popular belief, I seriously doubt it. The precise mechanisms enabling demons to sow doubt about God or feed evil in the hearts of men and women are probably linked to very complex social and psychological processes. Demons probably work in some sort of unholy partnership with a variety of means to promote evil. I will not speculate any further about these mechanisms since their part in the anti-God "global conspiracy" is probably ultimately indistinguishable from the so-called "natural" factors we can ascertain directly. The only thing we can be certain of is that these evil beings' actions are real, and they are seamlessly entangled in the historical mechanisms that give substance to the evil intrinsic in the human heart.

In other words, demonic beings need a framework or a support system to do their work in the world; they cannot fan the flames of evil in a vacuum. This support system is the human social web.

While I believe demons play an important role in promoting evil in the world, I do not think demons can bear the main responsibility for the evil we commit. Though they represent radical evil, and though they may somehow use various human mechanisms to promote their agenda, they cannot force us to embrace evil. In fact, their ability to influence us without our consent is extremely limited.

Whether some people embrace radical evil because they were abused as children, or have read Nietzsche or Hitler's *Mein Kampf*, or embraced Satanism, ultimately, as Scripture repeatedly asserts, *the responsibility is theirs alone*.

Positively stated, regardless of the extent of one's depravity, and the extent to which one has given oneself to satanic beings, we do know that while there is life, this person retains the ability to turn to God. We know this because Scripture tells us it is so. [13] The Bible also tells us that God, through his Spirit,

---

13   The story of the demon-possessed man in Mark 5, reviewed in Chapter 3, is an excellent case in point.

constantly draws us to him. These two factors mitigate the impact of the social environment and our own innate tendency towards evil.

In the end, the determining final factor is the human will. Ultimately, each of us bears the final responsibility for the choices we make. This may explain one question Christians ask regarding the relationship between Christ's victory at the cross and the continued activity of demonic beings. If, as the New Testament states, Christ has gained absolute victory over sin and death, why are the effects of that victory not more evident in respect to Satan and his minions? Beside the fact that human history is now in a transition period in which the human race has an opportunity to accept God's invitation, the reality is that in this transitional period, the power of Satan is severely curtailed but our ability to choose is not! As long as the human race remains in its present state, the devil continues to have power because humans still have the potential to believe in him. They can still give their allegiance to him and to everything he represents.

Question #3: Why does demon-possession seem to be that much more prevalent in non-Western or animistic cultures?

In case there is any doubt about this question's legitimacy, the underlying assumption is correct: Missionaries who have served in non-Western or animistic cultures generally attest to the reality of a greater prevalence of blatant and visible cases of demon-possession in such societies.

To explain this reality, I would like to highlight two general assumptions. First, that there are spirit beings wholly dedicated to opposing God and promoting evil on earth. Second, that these entities can interact with people to the extent that they, individually or as a culture, welcome, embrace or give allegiance to these spirits, either directly or indirectly. These assumptions explain to some extent why overt demon-possession or Satanic influence is a relatively rare phenomenon in Western societies and more prevalent in some others. Because we live in a culture that does not generally promote active allegiance to demons, their ability to directly control people is limited. While evil still thrives because of our ability to make moral choices, the power of demons is curtailed, hence the relative scarcity of blatant demon-possessed cases.

Basically, this is a worldview issue.[14] In cultures that either deny or simply ignore the demonic, the overt influence of evil spirits tends to be significantly restricted. Demons, as we noted in the Gospel of Mark and in 1 Corinthians, have very little power in and of themselves. Whatever power they have is essentially derived from the men and women they prey on. But in settings where spirits are actively worshiped, solicited and entreated, demon-possession will be an ever-present reality. The ultimate impact such a spirit-centered worldview has on that society—including the extent of destruction, human abuse, economic disruption and violence— will essentially hinge upon the magnitude of demon worship amongst the general population in that culture.

It is first and foremost an issue of worldview!

The little-known Yanomamö people who live in the jungles of southern Venezuela represent one of the most dramatic examples of a culture in which the spirit world is the focal point of human existence. Mark Ritchie, in his book *Spirit of the Rainforest*, provides an extraordinary snapshot of the life of the Yanomamö.[15] What is most remarkable is the fact that the book's narrator is none other than a Yanomamö shaman. This is not just another anthropological essay.

The first chapters are jarring. *Spirit of the Rainforest* shatters the myth of the "noble savage" who, untouched by Western civilization, lives in perfect harmony with his natural environment. Extreme violence, fear of the spirits, hunger, insecurity, terror and death characterize the existence of the Yanomamö. This is a culture where violence and deception are glorified, where children are left to starve when food is in short supply, where women are little more than objects to be raped at will or brutally killed in fits of anger.

---

14 For a more detailed treatment of this question, see Paul G. Hiebert, "The Flaw of the Excluded Middle," in *Anthropological Reflections on Missiological Issues* (Grand Rapids, MI: Baker Books, 1994), 189-201; "Healing and the Kingdom of God," in *Anthropological Reflections*, 217-253. See also Jacob Loewen, "Demon Possession and Exorcism in Africa, in the New Testament Context and in North America," in *Essays on Spiritual Bondage and Deliverance, Occasional Papers No. 11* (Elkhart, IN: Institute of Mennonite Studies, 1988), 118-145.

15 Mark Ritchie, *Spirit of the Rainforest*, 2nd ed. (Chicago, IL: Island Lake Press, 2000 [1996]).

It is impossible for the reader to get an accurate picture of the Yanomamö culture's brutality without actually reading Ritchie's book. The most interesting dimension of this book is the description of the relationship between the Yanomamö and the spirit world. Jungleman, the Yanomamö shaman, describes how the spirits came to him while he was still a child and how his mother encouraged him to welcome them. He then speaks of these spirits who lived in his chest. He describes the intimate relationship he maintained with them: the conversations, the requests for advice, power for war and healing. One of the female spirits even served as a regular sexual partner! Jungleman describes a world that is entirely immersed in the spirit world.

The Yanomamö culture takes the existence of spirits for granted. As with Jungleman, spirits are actively sought by the shamans and welcomed in their chests, where they live in what appears to be some kind of symbiotic relationship. While most symbiotic relationships are beneficial to the host and the parasite, in this case, the relationship holds no net benefit for the host. These spirits' only purpose is to bolster the forces of violence, oppression and self-destruction that characterize the Yanomamö culture. Even more significantly, these spirits constantly tell the shamans that the one they call Yai Pada—the great spirit—hates the Yanomamö people and must be resisted at all costs.

Do the Yanomamö people need the spirits they worship to maintain a culture that preys on the weak and glorifies violence? Absolutely not! While these spirits are not necessarily the ultimate source of the self-destructive forces that undermine the Yanomamö culture, the account does support the notion that embracing such beings does result in focusing and amplifying the forces of self-destruction already present amongst the Yanomamö.

Question #4: What should Christians do if they think they have encountered a person who appears to be demon-possessed?

Although encountering demon-possessed people may not be all that frequent in countries like the United States or Canada, the fact remains that it can happen. The odds of such incidents will certainly increase dramatically in settings where people dabble in some form of occultism or spiritism, or in countries where animism and spirit worship are intrinsic parts of the culture.

I fully realize that there are Christians who will be highly skeptical about actual demon-possession, either because they are uncomfortable with the whole notion or because they assume that the symptoms that might indicate demonic presence are more appropriately diagnosed as neurological disorders.

To some extent, I can sympathize with such sentiments. The behavior one might associate with demon-possession is practically impossible to distinguish from symptoms that would otherwise indicate some kind of psychosis. From a clinical perspective, there is no medical protocol to discern the one from the other. Moreover, psychologically, there is something profoundly unsettling about accepting the possibility that a person might actually be demon-possessed. For most of us, this is such a foreign notion that we simply do not have adequate categories to deal with such a condition effectively. As a result, most pastoral and medical practitioners will automatically revert to a medical diagnosis in such situations.

While I recognize the inherent difficulties of discerning the presence of evil spirits, and while I agree that a medical diagnostic might in most cases be the correct one, to reduce the notion of demon-possession to a neurological disorder does not represent an appropriate course of action. As we have seen in the examples in Mark's Gospel, the New Testament leaves no doubt about the reality of demonic beings and their ability to "infect" and adversely affect human beings. To systematically resort to a psychological paradigm as a universal explanation for all apparent cases of demonic possession does not adequately reflect the New Testament data.

While the New Testament supports the possibility that real cases of demon-possession cases can emerge anywhere, I do not believe Christians should necessarily initiate an elaborate ritual to exorcise the demons. If a suspected case of demon-possession emerges, I would first advise great caution in diagnosing and intervening.

We often forget that human beings have an enormous capacity for a wide range of behavior. Some people have, for lack of a better expression, odd personalities and matching behavior patterns. Others may have given in to their evil impulses. There are people, for example, who become extremely violent under the influence of alcohol. Others suffer from various kinds of temporary or chronic mental disorders. And then, there are those who might truly be under the influence of demonic forces. To complicate matters even more, evil behavior may be a combination of many of these factors; none of them should be discounted.

In cases where demonic possession is strongly suspected, many spiritual warfare practitioners will resort to a practice known as "power encounter." This expression is used in a number of ways. In his *Handbook for Spiritual Warfare*, Ed Murphy provides a very helpful summary of the various ways it has been understood. In some cases, power encounter is equated with evangelism in the sense that men and women are released from Satan's power into the power of God.[16] Others associate power encounter with Christian living: The entire Christian life is perceived as a power encounter that resists Satan and the forces of evil.[17] John Wimber associates power encounter with miracles, signs and wonders. Any event where the kingdom of God confronts the kingdom of this world is a power encounter, particularly when it involves exorcisms and healings.[18] Ed Murphy proposes a wide-ranging definition that encompasses all the others. He sees power encounter as "a crisis point of encounter in the ongoing spiritual warfare between the two supernatural kingdoms..." [19]

Arriving at a final definition of power encounter is of little relevance here. I am mostly concerned with those who understand power encounters to be what I would describe as aggressive exorcism "showdowns." Typically, these sessions involve a person who manifests a behavior denoting demonic influence, such as chronic depression, obscene speech, an inability to go to church, read the Bible or talk about spiritual matters. It may include an uncontrollable fear of spirits, paranoia, hearing voices, an intense desire to commit suicide or to kill others.

The actual "showdown" itself can be quite elaborate and traumatic for all concerned. The person suspected of demon-possession is brought into a private space, typically a home or a room in a church. A number of people

---

16   See Murphy, *The Handbook for Spiritual Warfare*, 341.

17   Murphy, *The Handbook of Spiritual Warfare*, 341-342.

18   Murphy, *The Handbook of Spiritual Warfare*, 342.

19   Murphy, *The Handbook of Spiritual Warfare*, 342.

participate in such power encounters. At least one church leader with some experience in demon-casting is usually present. Friends or relatives may be on hand as well. Though the exact protocol for these kinds of sessions varies, the following approach proposed by Roy Matheson, Professor Emeritus of New Testament at Tyndale Seminary, reflects the practice well. Matheson typically assembles a small team of four to five people composed of professionals and non-professionals.

The session itself begins with prayer and praise to ensure victory and to ask for protection for both the "client" and the team. Matheson also recommends asking the Holy Spirit to give discernment as the team proceeds with the exorcism. The next step consists of commanding the spirits causing the manifestations to stop immediately. This is important to demonstrate to the spirits who is in charge. Next, Matheson commands the strongest spirit or spirits to reveal their names, and then they are expelled from the demon-possessed person. Sometimes, the spirits' names can be gathered by asking the afflicted person directly. These spirits must be expelled by name and told never to return. Following this, Matheson suggests doing a final check to ensure that all the spirits have gone away.[20] This method or variations thereof characterize deliverance sessions otherwise known as power encounters.

I think it is generally preferable to avoid this type of elaborate intervention. First and most importantly, this approach tends to over-dramatize the issue and ends up attributing much more power to demons than the New Testament does. As I pointed out in the section on the Gospel of Mark, exorcism stories were not intended to provide a demon-casting protocol, but to expose an old lie about demonic powers. Though they are real, demons do not, as was commonly believed then, have overwhelming occult or magical powers over human beings. Quite the opposite. Their only power lies in the willingness of men and women to give themselves over.

The first and most serious error we can make when dealing with people who appear to be afflicted by demons is to engage them in a way that assumes the supernatural beings do in fact have extraordinary powers over them. They simply do not!

---

20 For more details, see Roy R. Matheson, "When You're in the War Zone. A View of Spiritual Warfare," *Christian Counseling Today*, Winter 1994.

Second, power encounters can get out of control when the demons do not appear to leave as easily as one might expect. The "client" begins to thrash around while making strange noises. The exorcists panic and become even more aggressive in their attempts to expel the demons. The power encounter can and sometimes does degenerate into a very dangerous situation. In some exceptional cases, it can even result in the death of the person being exorcised.[21]

If these demonic showdowns generally resulted in a dramatic disappearance of the symptoms, that would be cause enough for promoting them. But that is not the reality. Though power encounters may represent a healing catalyst for some, the symptoms that prompted the intervention in the first place do not necessarily vanish. As Matheson observes: "We have found that in most cases, further counseling will be needed."[22]

Here is where the power encounter can represent a grave danger to the person being exorcised. In cases where the symptoms remain, the tendency among many spiritual warfare interveners is to assume they are dealing with exceptionally powerful demons. Such an assumption can lead to very serious consequences for people who may in fact be suffering from a neurological condition. What these people need is not more elaborate attempts at casting out demons, but prompt medical support.

Readers might object that there is no easy way to determine whether we are dealing with demon possession or a psychological problem. While I sympathize with the concern, I would like to suggest an approach that I believe is most consistent with the theoretical model we have developed throughout this book, whatever the real problem might turn out to be—whether it is demon-possession or a chemical imbalance.

First, it is very important not to assume anything about the root cause of the symptoms the person is experiencing. While it is advisable to be open to the possibility of demon possession, particularly so when dealing

---

21 Suffice it to mention the recent case (August 2003) of a young autistic boy, Terrence Cottrell, who died while being held down by church members and a pastor during an exorcism BBC News, "Court Hears 'Exorcism' Death Case," BBC News, http://news.bbc.co.uk/1/hi/world/americas/3877421. stm (accessed July 8, 2004). Marguerite Shuster, in a very insightful article on the potential dangers of indiscriminate exorcisms, also addresses this issue in "Giving the Devil More Than His Due," *Leadership* 12 (1991):64-67.

22 See R. Matheson, "When You are in the War Zone," 24.

with a person who manifests overt spiritual hostility, I don't think one should commit to any diagnosis at this stage of the intervention.

Second, it is absolutely vital to gather as much information as possible about the individual. Get to know the afflicted person. People who struggle with serious psychological issues are profoundly distressed over what they are experiencing. They lack confidence and are prone to the wildest speculations about the cause of their distress. They are desperate to find a solution and thus very susceptible to being manipulated. This type of intervention should be performed with extreme sensitivity; with the utmost respect for the individual and, if possible, in the context of a meaningful relationship.

Third, it is important to remember that the objective of this kind of intervention is healing. If it means casting out demons to achieve that goal, so be it. If there are no demons, so much the better! Healing must remain the primary focus of the intervention. The New Testament does seem to confirm this intuition. Remarkably enough, particularly when we consider the culture of magic in which it emerged, the New Testament does not provide a formal protocol for casting out demons. The only formal procedure attested in the New Testament is found in the Book of James (5:13-16) and relates to physical and spiritual healing. In spite of its generic character, I believe the "James Protocol" can be very helpful for dealing with suspected cases of demon possession.

The formula proposed by James applies to people experiencing major health problems. Whether the ailments are of a physical or psychological character is irrelevant. The procedure does not presume on the real cause of the illness. In fact, a precise diagnosis appears unnecessary. The prayer for healing puts great emphasis on the patient's initiative and on the importance of the community, particularly the critical role of the leaders. "*Are any among you sick? They should call for the elders of the church and have them pray over them…*" (5:14). James encourages the person who is distressed by illness to seek the Christian community's help. This encouragement counteracts the tendency some people have to isolate themselves from others in difficult times.

The elders are specified because they represent the Christian community, and because of the greater degree of accountability that is intrinsic to their office. The unspoken assumption is that these leaders can offer mature and compassionate care. Though there is no way to be certain, James may have recommended an appeal to the church leaders, because there would be less likelihood of incompetence. This is a very important concern for people who are struggling with difficult personal issues and who therefore find themselves in a vulnerable position. Appealing to mature and responsible leaders is made even more necessary as this intervention is not meant to be a mechanical process or a simple ritual. The allusions to the forgiveness of sin (v.15) and mutual confession (v. 6) imply a framework of pastoral care that extends far beyond a simple appeal to physical healing. My earlier comments about the importance of entering into a personal relationship with the suffering person in fact derives in great part from James's own pastoral perspective on the ministry of healing.

This low key approach has a number of advantages over the more aggressive showdown method generally favored by demonic warfare specialists. First, the James 5 method does not seek to immediately identify the person's exact problem. It leaves all the options open. Second, this approach does not empower demons. We have seen in our study of Mark and 1 Corinthians that demonic beings are ontologically powerless. The powers they enjoy come from the belief system of a culture or individuals with whom they interact. The prayer of healing does not at all preclude praying for demonic deliverance. I do strongly recommend that demons be explicitly cast out, but that the prayer for deliverance be framed within the broader context of healing. Third, the James formula appeals to the individual's sense of responsibility. Those who are sick must call the elders; they must take ownership of their own situation and seek help from the Christian community. The intervention cannot be unilaterally foisted upon them. Fourth, this approach assumes the participation of leaders who are accountable to the broader Christian community, thus decreasing the risks of spiritual abuse. Fifth, this method ensures that the intervention is explicitly embedded within a thoughtful, balanced and compassionate pastoral framework. It should also be noted that the "burden of faith," as it were, is on the elders, not the person seeking help. Too often, the "patient" is blamed for not having sufficient faith when instantaneous healing does not occur. James reminds the reader that it is, in the end, the faith of the leaders that is at stake: "*The prayer of faith will save the sick, …*" (5:15).

In addition, this approach deals with one of the most acute and problematic dimensions of the deliverance ministry, i.e., the issue of diagnosis. How can we effectively distinguish between demon possession and mental illness? The answer may be much simpler than what most spiritual warfare specialists propose. If we take seriously what the Gospel of Mark and 1 Corinthians teach about demons, then the prayer of healing should be more than adequate to cast them out, if that is indeed part or the whole of the problem. Whether there is a dramatic manifestation of demonic deliverance or not is irrelevant. The prayer of healing will effectively deliver the person from demons. If the "patient's" difficulties are even partly caused by demonic influence, the demonic factor can be eliminated following the prayer of healing. Thus, the pastoral care provider can rule out continued demonic influence.

If, however, the person still exhibits the same symptoms after the prayer of healing, then we must assume an overt medical issue and immediately seek psychiatric support. Even if there is a combination of demonic and neurological issues, the prayer of healing rules out continued demonic influence and allows the elders to address other factors that may be at play. From this point on, we can be assured that we are not dealing with demon possession any longer, but with a psychological or neurological condition that requires counseling or medical attention.

It may sound too simple for some, but this is where the biblical evidence leads. The approach should hold true in the vast majority of cases except perhaps when dealing with people who have been involved in the occult and have no intention of abandoning their demonic practices and Satanic allegiance. The James Protocol assumes that the person seeking relief wants not only healing, but also a genuine relationship with God. The effectiveness of the prayer of healing is absolutely contingent on the person's willingness to seek God and be loyal to him.

There is a major problem in assuming the presence of stubborn spirits when the deliverance procedure does not immediately lead to a dramatic improvement (which incidentally, appears to be more the norm than the exception). Rather than shifting strategy, the deliverance team simply puts their effort into the demon-casting cycle all over again. I cannot overemphasize the risks inherent to this outlook. It may dangerously postpone medical attention. In the case of people struggling with clinical depression, delay may even lead to a suicide attempt.

A few years ago, I met a young woman who had begun to exhibit psychotic symptoms and suicidal tendencies at the age of 16. The symptoms were quite ominous. She could hear voices that allegedly revealed her classmates' secret thoughts. She was convinced her whole family had been abducted and replaced by alien clones. Her suspicions even included her own dog. Her mother felt that we were perhaps dealing with demonic oppression. We prayed the prayer of healing for her, including an explicit request that demons be cast out. There was no marked improvement. In fact, her symptoms worsened. At that point, I was certain that her condition was not related to any demonic presence. I counseled that the young woman be immediately brought to a doctor, who prescribed anti-depressant and anti-psychotic drugs. Within three weeks, the symptoms had all but disappeared. While she remains on small doses of the medications and is still being monitored by a psychiatrist, she manages to live a productive life. At the very least, the psychosis is under control and her mood disorder is manageable.

Was this young woman under demonic influence? From what we could observe, it is very unlikely that she was. Had the root cause of her condition been demonic, the demons would have immediately left her and the symptoms would have disappeared. The reality is that, after the prayer of healing, this young woman still suffered from the same problems. According to the framework I have developed throughout this book, this could only mean that the problem was other than demonic. So we moved to "Plan B" and consulted a psychiatrist to obtain a medical follow up.

Question #5: What about Ancestral Curses?

Recently I did a television interview in which I commented at length on a number of Old Testament issues. At some point in the discussion, we touched on the whole area of magic and curses in the Bible.[23] Afterward a woman who was struggling with severe migraines and whose family had a similar history e-mailed me and asked whether she and her family

---

23 Much of the interest I have in this topic relates to my Ph. D. dissertation, which dealt with the use and function of the curse motif in the pre-exilic prophets (Le motif imprécatoire chez les prophètes bibliques du 8e siècle A.C. à la lumière du Proche-Orient ancien [Université de Montréal, 1993]).

could be victims of an ancestral curse. Based on Exodus 34:6-7, where it states that God *"but visiting the iniquity of the parents upon the children and the children's children, to the third and the fourth generation,"*[24] she had surmised that her family might be under the influence of a generational curse as a result of sin in her ancestral past. That being a possibility, a friend suggested she go through a program of "generational cleansing" through an organization called Ray of Hope Ministries,[25] founded by Rev. Ray McGraw in 1989.

The basic idea behind a generational cleansing is simple. To perform such a procedure, the person must prepare a family tree, note all the known sin issues in the family, confess them and pray for healing. While this woman was obviously hoping this procedure would eliminate her migraines, she also wanted to know whether it was a justifiable practice from a biblical perspective.

Beyond her specific question about ancestral curses, the broader issue of curses is quite confounding. Much of that confusion, however, is the result of misconceptions about the nature of curses in the Old Testament. Too many people equate the biblical curse with the type of curse cultivated in popular culture and, to some extent, promoted by spiritual warfare specialists.

The Old Testament curse always results from a clearly stated injunction (Gen. 2:15-17; 3:1-7). In the covenant context, the curse and the blessing are direct consequences of disobedience or obedience to the terms of the covenant. Unlike big-budget Hollywood productions that portray curses as terrifying forces unleashed by the careless actions of inept characters, Old Testament curses are remarkably straightforward and upfront. If the people violated the injunctions of the covenant, particularly as it pertained to idolatry, they would have to live with the consequences of their disobedience. Usually these curses are couched in the language of natural catastrophes or defeat in war (Lev. 26 and Deut. 27-28). In the Old Testament, the curse is primarily an expression of God's judgment.

---

24   See also Exod. 20:5; 34:6-7; Num. 14:18; Matt. 23:31-35.

25   For more information, consult the organization's website at http://www.rayofhopeministries. com/index.htm (accessed October 1, 2007).

You shall not bow down to them or worship them; for I the LORD your God am a jealous God, punishing children for the iniquity of parents, to the third and the fourth generation of those who reject me, but showing steadfast love to the thousandth generation of those who love me and keep my commandments (Exod. 20:5-6).

Such passages in no way suggest that some automatic, mechanical or magical principle governs the curse's implementation. By contrasting the extent of the blessing to a "thousandth generation" with the punishment's reach to the third and fourth generation, the author actually emphasizes the grace of God. This text shows that God will judge disobedience and that his judgment may impact his people over a number of generations. In contrast, if the people obeyed, they would enjoy God's blessings over a thousand generations.

The notion that a curse upon one's family history may work itself out in some mysterious or magical fashion has no basis in Scripture. This kind of belief is incompatible with the Bible's teachings, mainly because of the worldview that would be necessary to support such a belief. In the ancient world, magical powers depended on the intervention of the gods. Genesis 1 clearly states that there are no gods except Elohim. If there are no gods, then magic, as generally understood, can not exist. We can, therefore, extrapolate from Genesis 1 the absence of a cosmic substructure that would enable magical practices or the transmission of curses. The only curses the Old Testament recognizes as efficient are those uttered and implemented by the power of God.

What does that mean for "generational cleansing"? Should such a practice be avoided? In and of itself, the practice is probably harmless. One could even argue that the ritual might bring a degree of psychological relief and could act like a spiritual placebo or a healing catalyst. Even if that were the case, I would argue for a complete avoidance of such a practice. Besides the fact that there is no trace of such a custom in the Bible, the theological assumptions underlying this ritual have no biblical support at all. The procedure clearly derives from a misinterpretation of a number of Old Testament texts and assumes a magical framework that is utterly incompatible with the biblical worldview outlined in the Creation account.

From a practical point of view, the suggested protocol is impossible to implement in any meaningful way. Generational cleansing not only requires articulating a detailed family tree, it also assumes that the person engaged in this practice is able to identify the ancestral sins that may have opened the door to demonic spirits. Even if a person could produce a sufficiently detailed family tree, identifying which people might have committed the kind of actions that would result in creating demonic strongholds in the family line is essentially impossible and ultimately futile.

While some readers might still argue for using generational cleansing as a psychological therapeutic measure, I am convinced we never bring meaningful help to anyone by appealing to concepts or procedures that do not reflect our best understanding of the truth. Even if some things appear to be helpful in the short term, there is always a price to pay in the long term. Jesus said it is the truth that would make us free, not wishful thinking.

Furthermore, if the generational cleansing fails to improve the person's condition—as will unavoidably and too often be the case—it will likely be blamed on an inadequate ancestral investigation. Individuals who find themselves in a weakened psychological or medical state may in fact spiral out of control as they obsessively attempt to identify the ancestral sin at the root of their difficulties. I recommend that people who are worried about ancestral sins as the possible cause of a serious ailment focus on seeking spiritual support—by appealing to church leaders to perform the prayer of healing—and medical help.

A Few Final and Sobering Words

This book on demonic warfare is much more than just another study on demons. It is partly an attempt to address the puzzling loss of confidence in the most basic tenets of the Judeo-Christian worldview our society is presently experiencing and to challenge the rise of pantheism and animism in our culture. But most fundamentally, this book is an essay in biblical theology; an encouragement for Christians to think about their world from a biblical foundation. *Ultimately, this book is a plea for a return to Text and Reason.*

In this concluding section, I wish to offer some final observations about three critical issues. First, a word of clarification about a question that is extremely problematic for many and is still a source of much controversy: What is the precise extent of demonic power? Second, I am aware of the excruciating challenges faced by pastors and missionaries who work in traditional cultures. The second part of this chapter outlines a road map which I hope will give concrete assistance to those who serve on the front lines. And third, I want to remind the reader that demonic manifestation is not the monopoly of non-Western cultures. As stated in the Introduction, there is something sinister happening in the Western world. I am increasingly convinced we are experiencing an ideological shift that is preparing the hearts and minds of this generation to open the door to entities eager to feed on and focus the evil already within us.

Do Demons Have Real Power?

People often challenge my assertion that demons have no real powers. To clarify, I contend that demons are real entities with no power over the physical universe. Since the Creation account leaves no space for magical or occult forces, it follows that demons, though real, cannot enjoy any effective power over the physical world. Not only does the Creation account propose a plausibility structure that annihilates the possibility of magical or occult forces, both the Gospel of Mark and Paul's first epistle to the Corinthians confirm the status of demons as empty shadows.[1]

Demons are real, but their reality is mere illusion in the presence of the absolute reality of God. Real power and substance can only be derived from God. Outside of him, there can only be a mere whisper of reality. By

---

1 For more details, see Chapter 3.

virtue of their rebellious position, demons can only exhibit an infinitesimal degree of reality and substance. This is not to say these evil entities are harmless. The New Testament and human experience attest that under certain conditions, they can be extremely destructive, particularly when they are given the opportunity to wield their only power: the power of persuasion.

The most basic inclination of these evil entities is to oppose God and generate chaos in the world. But their power to do so is ultimately contingent on our willingness to consciously embrace these spirits or espouse the ideologies of death and chaos upon which they feed. The power of demons ultimately hinges on the belief system of the culture in which they navigate. This factor accounts for the variations in the frequency and intensity of overt demonic manifestations between cultures. The prevalence of demonic manifestations in Africa, Haiti or India, and their relative and apparent scarcity in the Western world are linked to a worldview that cultivates belief and interaction with spirits in the former but generally ignores their existence in the latter.

Demons can only terrorize those who attribute such power to them. In that respect, the Third Wave model is extremely problematic. It tends to perpetuate a common and dangerous misperception of the demonic world. By structurally reproducing a non-biblical model, it inadvertently and ironically reinforces a worldview that offers a false representation of the physical universe, resulting in the empowerment of demonic forces. While there is grave danger in negating the existence of demons, we must not underestimate the risks associated with articulating a "Christianized form of animism in which spirits and magic are used to explain everything."[2]

Demons do not have the power to infect human beings without their consent or to unilaterally impose their agenda upon people. These beings, however, can exert catastrophic influence over those who willingly seek them. Never forget Adolf Hitler. He was only a determined small man with a bad temper. Yet, he managed to captivate enough people to affect the course of history. Somehow, demons have the ability to prey on the evil inclinations of the human heart, focus them, amplify their impact on the very people they oppress, and facilitate the diffusion of evil throughout

---

2 Hiebert, "Excluded Middle," 200

human society. This is the grave danger that threatens Western culture. As we move further and further away from the Judeo-Christian worldview, we will increasingly become subject to adopting a worldview that progressively gives ever-greater credence to the supernatural and, by extension, to the powers of demons.

A Proposal for Missionaries

How missionaries should address demonic phenomena in animistic or traditional cultures has long been a controversial topic.[3] As the Christian anthropologist, Paul Hiebert, states in his important article, "The Flaw of the Excluded Middle," many missiologists and missionaries experience a high degree of ambivalence in their efforts to reconcile their belief in rationality and empirical science with the apparent reality and predominance of magic and occult phenomena in many non-Western societies. Incidentally, the same could be said of church leaders who are being confronted with the rise of the New Age movement in Europe and North America. This ambivalence is best revealed in the divergent interpretations of illnesses and other afflictions in settings where missionaries are in contact with cultures that have not assimilated the Western worldview and the scientific method.

The dilemma missionaries face is not uncommon. As Hiebert readily points out, such ideological tensions regularly occur whenever native Christians and Western missionaries face traditional beliefs and practices. His observations on the conceptual incongruity experienced by recent Christian converts as they attempt to calibrate their response to traditional healers are revealing:

> What happens to villagers who become Christians? Most of them take problems they formerly took to the saints to the Christian minister or missionary. Christ replaces Krishna or Siva as the healer of spiritual diseases. Many of them in time turn to Western allopathic medicines for many of the illnesses they had taken to the doctor and quack. But what of the plagues that the magician cured? What about spirit possession or curses or witchcraft or black magic? What is the Christian answer to these?[4]

---

3   Hiebert, "Excluded Middle," 189-201.
4   Hiebert, "Excluded Middle," 191.

Hiebert's subsequent comments highlight the heart of the dilemma and the issue that leaves so many Christian leaders without a place to stand.

> Often the missionary evangelist or doctor has no answer. These do not really exist, they say. But to people for whom these are very real experiences in their lives, there must be another answer. Therefore, many of them return to the magician for cures.
>
> This survival of magic among Christians is not unique to India. In many parts of the world, the picture is the same. In the West, magic and witchcraft persisted well into the seventeenth century, more than a thousand years after the gospel came to these lands. [5]

For Hiebert, the heart of the issue is the fundamental differences in how the various worldviews are articulated. On the one hand, we have the traditional religionists who view the physical world in an "organic" fashion, "in terms of living beings in relationship to one another."[6] Hiebert further describes it as an animistic worldview, a world he characterizes as "relational" rather than "deterministic." On the other hand, the Western worldview is portrayed as "mechanistic."[7] "Western sciences see the world as made up of lifeless matter that interacts on the basis of forces." [8] A model he further describes as "deterministic."[9]

Although one could debate whether organic/relational and mechanistic/deterministic are the best terms to describe these plausibility structures, Hiebert's criticism of the Western worldview is essentially correct. It offers no categories to deal effectively with what he calls the "middle-level" issues. This chasm between traditional religion and Western science has often left missionaries empty-handed when dealing with the animistic dimensions of the cultures to which they were to bring the Gospel. Hiebert writes,

> As a scientist I had been trained to deal with the empirical world in naturalistic terms. As a theologian I was taught to answer ultimate questions in theistic terms. For me the middle zone did not exist. Unlike the Indian villagers, I had given little thought to spirits of this

---

5 Hiebert, "Excluded Middle," 191-193.
6 Hiebert, "Excluded Middle," 195.
7 Hiebert, "Excluded Middle," 195-196.
8 Hiebert, "Excluded Middle," 195.
9 Hiebert, "Excluded Middle," 195.

world, to local ancestors and ghosts, or to the souls of animals. For me these belonged to the realm of fairies, trolls, and other mythical beings. Consequently I had no answers to the questions they raised…" [10]

Hiebert's critique of missionary activity is caustic:

It should be apparent why many missionaries trained in the West had no answers to the problems of the middle level—they often did not even see it. When tribal people spoke of fear of evil spirits, they denied the existence of the spirits rather than claim the power of Jesus Christ over them. The result, Lesslie Newbigin has argued, is that Western Christian missions have been one of the greatest secularizing forces in history. [11]

The consequences of this conceptual deficiency have been and continue to be devastating for Christian outreach. If the missionary has no answers to the culture's critical issues, the intended audience will either view Christianity as a woefully inadequate option or, if they embrace the Christian faith, they will eventually, as Hiebert points out, return to the "diviner who gives definite answers." [12]

Hiebert refuses to leave the question unanswered and proposes a theological model outline that comprehensively deals with all aspects of human existence. His proposal is helpful, adequately reflecting the essential elements of what a Christian worldview should address. [13]

An Issue of Clarity and Confidence

I concur with Hiebert's description of the missionary dilemma, but I am not convinced that the missionaries' inability to deal effectively with traditional beliefs lies in their uncritical adherence to modernist

---

10   Hiebert, "Excluded Middle," 196.

11   Hiebert, "Excluded Middle," 197.

12   Hiebert, "Excluded Middle," 198.

13   Hiebert views the development of an adequate theological model on three levels. On the highest level, it should include a theology of God in cosmic history: creation, redemption, purpose and destiny. On the middle level, it includes a theology of God in human history: divine guidance, provision, healing, pain and suffering. On the lowest level, it includes an awareness of God in natural history in sustaining the natural order of things ("Excluded Middle," 199).

assumptions. For one thing, thoroughgoing modernists don't become missionaries! Most missionaries believe in God, prayer and the power of the Holy Spirit. They believe in God's ability to perform miracles and to intervene in human history. In this respect, Hiebert's diagnosis needs further calibration.

My assessment of the problem is slightly different. The difficulty does not derive as much from an undiscriminating concession to Western assumptions as from a lack of clarity about the biblical worldview and how it addresses the supernatural. This ideological uncertainty eventually results in a chronic lack of confidence, which has led missionaries to deal with animism and spiritism in one of two ways. Some simply refuse to take a firm position in regards to the more explicitly animistic elements of the culture. These people are not necessarily parsing the assumptions of a scientific model that characterizes the universe in mechanistic terms. They are simply unsure of their own premises and cannot decisively deal with traditional beliefs. Others have chosen to deal with magic and superstition by completely adopting the assumptions of the Third Wave movement.

Either one of these approaches entails severe difficulties. The first fails to address serious cultural and spiritual realities. The second may result in legitimizing beliefs that do not adequately reflect a biblical theological framework and may contribute to effectively creating models that exhibit various degrees of syncretism or, as Hiebert puts it, "Christianized animism."[14] How can we intelligently avoid one extreme or the other? While Hiebert's article spells out the problem and hints at a possible solution, his proposal remains too tentative to concretely assist missionaries who need a clear strategy to address urgent and critical issues.

A Strategic Road Map

The road map I propose can provide a starting point for addressing traditional beliefs. First, missionaries must learn to focus on the issue of worldview. They need to precisely determine what constitutes the biblical worldview and be in a position to parse its implications for an animistic culture.

---

14   Hiebert, "Excluded Middle," p. 200.

I cannot overemphasize the importance of this first step and the need to engage in this exercise independent of the issue of cultural sensitivity. Analytical work and cultural respect are both essential aspects of missionary activity, but they must not be arbitrarily intermingled. While missionaries are well advised to avoid unnecessary cause for offense, it is paramount to distinguish between critical analysis and outreach strategy. The first step is an academic exercise that articulates the basic structure of the biblical worldview, analyzes the plausibility structure of the culture, and compares the two in order to highlight similarities and differences. Then and only then can missionaries be in a position to develop the best strategy to confront their audience with the biblical claims.

Too often, I observe the reverse. We allow matters of cultural sensitivity to cloud our analytical work and dictate our conclusions. The more political freight is tied to an issue or a particular people group, the greater this threat becomes. We should never let the potential for offense dictate our search for truth. As a colleague wisely said to me once, "...but what is society missing in its search for truth and what are we missing when we let society dictate our [the Christian academic community] priorities?"

The first and foremost concern of the Christian thinker is to discern truth and confront the world with its claims. If we consciously or unconsciously fail to fulfill this task, there is no compelling purpose for us. We become just one more meaningless voice in the cacophony of post-modernity. We need to take to heart God's warning to Ezekiel:

> *If I say to the wicked, "O wicked ones, you shall surely die," and you do not speak to warn the wicked to turn from their ways, the wicked shall die in their iniquity, but their blood I will require at your hand. But if you warn the wicked to turn from their ways, and they do not turn from their ways, the wicked shall die in their iniquity, but you will have saved your life (Ezek. 33:8-9).*

Second, missionaries must consciously and intentionally choose to trust in the most basic concepts of the biblical worldview. The relationship between exegesis and biblical theology, on the one hand, and "practice,"[15]

---

15 I never feel completely comfortable using the term "practical" to denote praxis. Whether it is explicitly formulated or not, ministry practices and skills always assume, require and express a theoretical framework.

on the other, needs to be more linear. In a sense, the methodology found in a field like engineering, where the relationship between theory and application is indeed linear, is an approach that may prove helpful for practitioners and theorists. When an engineer builds a bridge, there is an absolute certainty regarding the load such a structure can carry. There is nothing haphazard about bridge building; the process is based on scientific principles that are implicitly trusted.

I realize that some of my readers will dismiss me as unbearably naive and impossibly unsophisticated, epistemologically speaking. In this post-modern era, it is no longer fashionable to think in terms of a body of truth that functions as an absolute point of reference. But, as with many other things, post-modernism will eventually prove to be another fad that will collapse under its own epistemological inner contradictions. If more Christian academics could exhibit a little more resolve in this area, perhaps we could have a significant influence on the ideological devolution of the Western world. I for one refuse to get on that sinking ship.[16] Once we have ascertained with a reasonable measure of certitude the outline of a biblical worldview, we should move with confidence.

As Hiebert has shown, the issue of magic and occult practices is a source of much vexation for missionaries who, for the most part, tend to have a very equivocal stance towards those practices and their underlying assumptions. The question, however, that needs clarification is remarkably simple: Is there *real* magic in the world and is there any physical reality to the powers behind occult practices? Judging from the near-consensus found in the spiritual warfare literature, the vastly popular appeal of the *Left Behind* series, and the fascination for the occult and the New Age in popular culture, a majority of lay people, missionaries and other practitioners would probably answer in the affirmative.[17]

---

16 Those who wish to pursue this further can consult Alvin Plantinga, "*Christian Philosophy at the End of the Twentieth Century,*" in *Christian Philosophy at the Close of the Twentieth Century,* ed. by Sander Griffioen and Bert Balk (Kampen, Netherlands: Kok, 1995), 329-353.

17 See Richard Kyle, The *Religious Fringe: A History of Alternative Religions in America* (Downers Grove, IL: InterVarsity Press, 1993) and *The New Age Movement in American Culture* (University Press of America, 1995). Stanley J. Grenz is atypical of where many Christians stand on the issue of magic and the occult. While he acknowledges the reality of demons and the absolute necessity to abstain from engaging in superstitious activities, he also believes that these "powers" are non-realities. Though the rationale proposed is not as clear as one might wish, Grenz is nevertheless among the few who attempt to distinguish between the ontological reality of demonic beings and the actual efficacy of their powers (see Stanley J. Grenz, "Superstition: A Christian Perspective," *The Asia Journal of Theology,* vol. 8 [1994]: 365-378).

In this book, I have argued against the intrinsic reality of an underlying psychic power grid in the universe. I am not suggesting we live in a world where miraculous acts never occur. The biblical witness certainly records many instances of such, not the least of which is the resurrection of Jesus Christ. But these supernatural acts are exclusively within the purview of God's intervention in history. [18]

The Power of Belief

If the Genesis Creation account provides an accurate portrait of reality, then the missionary must be willing to follow the assumptions set out in Genesis 1-3 to their logical conclusion. For instance, while a voodoo curse may have a devastating impact on a villager, the missionary must always remember that this apparent effect is brought about, not through an underlying grid of psychic (or demonic) energy, but through the power of suggestion, which can be as lethal as a loaded gun for people who embrace that culture's assumptions. For those who are prisoners of such a worldview and the evil entities that amplify it in the hearts and minds of the people they inhabit, the occult powers of the voodoo priest can be as real as the sun in the sky. The missionary, however, need not entertain such fears. Any ambivalence on their part should immediately trigger a reexamination of the biblical data.

Once the missionary has articulated a clear theoretical foundation, a strategic plan can be developed that incorporates a thorough knowledge of the people group in order to address the issue of cultural superstition. There are no easy formulas to determine the best approach to adopt. But at the very least, those who convert to Christianity should be introduced to the Creation account and given the opportunity to integrate its basic teachings.

A clear mind, disciplined by biblical theology, is the only sure way to immunize ourselves against falsehood and fear. Let's take to heart Paul's exhortation in Romans 12:2: *"Don't copy the behavior and customs of this world, but let God transform you into a new person by changing the way*

---

18 Those who wish to explore this issue further can consult C. S. Lewis, *Miracles* (New York, NY: Macmillan, 1947).

you think. Then you will learn to know God's will for you, which is good and pleasing and perfect" (NLT).

The Rise of the Gods

No one can read this book and remain indifferent. Either the reader will enthusiastically embrace its thesis, be profoundly troubled and challenged by it, or oppose it vehemently. There is limited ground for neutral indifference. Either demons exist or they don't. If they do, they can either affect men and women by manipulating forces beyond human control or they can't. Either there are real occult forces in the universe or there are none. There is no middle ground.

As Western society increasingly shuns the Judeo-Christian worldview to embrace ever-new versions of pantheism, a belief system C. S. Lewis aptly singled out as the "permanent natural bent of the human mind,"[19] the Church has an extraordinary opportunity to challenge a resurging ancient ideology that will only leave death and chaos if unopposed. If Lewis was right and pantheism has "in the long run, only one really formidable opponent—namely Christianity," then the Church must confidently and enthusiastically oppose it by displaying the portrait of reality found in the Genesis Creation account and parsed in the rest of Scripture.

The ideological universe abhors a vacuum. If the Judeo-Christian worldview is evacuated from Western culture, pantheism will resurface with a vengeance. Should that happen, belief in magic, occult forces, spirits and demonic entities will once again emerge from the murky waters of the human heart. The old gods never die. When Christianity suppresses them, they only bid their time until the season is ripe to rise again and do what they do best: create chaos, suffering and death.

The so-called post-modernism of our times is, I believe, an early expression of the ideological confusion that is increasingly characterizing Western societies. I am convinced the Age of the gods is once again upon us. If this generation of theologians and church leaders fail in opposing its rise, the slide towards animism and superstition will only get steeper and increasingly more difficult to resist.

---

19 Lewis, *Miracles*, 101.

G. K. Chesterton once wrote: "When men stop believing in God they don't believe in nothing; they believe in anything." We are now witnessing the awful veracity of this harsh observation. It is becoming increasingly clear to me that the Western world is enthusiastically embracing an ancient ideology of death. The signs of the death spiral in which we are engaged are everywhere.

Is there hope? Of course there is hope. Our destiny is not written in the stars; it is in our hands. We have a God-given ability to exercise our free will and determine our future. But whatever hope we have now resides in three things: 1) a commitment to the biblical text; 2) a determined choice to resist death's siren call; 3) an unconditional decision to turn back to the Living God.

No herd of demons can, not even for an instant, stand in the way of those who wish to embrace the source of all life and reality: Jesus Christ.

He is the image of the invisible God, the firstborn of all creation; for in him all things in heaven and on earth were created, things visible and invisible, whether thrones or dominions or rulers or powers— all things have been created through him and for him. He himself is before all things, and in him all things hold together. He is the head of the body, the church; he is the beginning, the firstborn from the dead, so that he might come to have first place in everything. For in him all the fullness of God was pleased to dwell, and through him God was pleased to reconcile to himself all things, whether on earth or in heaven, by making peace through the blood of his cross (Col. 1:15-20).

Appendix

Difficult Texts

Much of the thesis outlined in this book centers on the idea that only God has the ability to affect the physical universe in a supernatural manner. In other words, according to my proposed theological framework, there is no reality whatsoever to occult magic, and demons have no effective powers over the physical universe or unwilling human beings.

Understandably, such claims do present some problems for those who have witnessed what they would qualify as supernatural events, or for those who believe there are in fact biblical instances that explicitly challenge the assertions I make in my book. I have no way to either prove or disprove the testimonies of those who claim to have witnessed paranormal phenomena, beyond what people like James Randi and others have done to verify such claims. It is, however, important to examine some scriptural texts that seem to support the reality of magic or challenge my thesis that demons have little effective power.

Magic in the Bible

There are a number of Old Testament and New Testament passages that appear to give credence to the reality of magical phenomena.

Old Testament Passages[1]
1. Forbidden Practices (Deut. 18:10-14 [2])

Deuteronomy 18:10-14 refers to a number of magical practices of the ancient world such as divination, soothsaying, casting spells, seeking oracles from the dead, etc. The injunction to avoid such practices is reiterated various times in the Old Testament. The presence of such injunctions does not necessarily imply that the author believes in the effective power of these practices. At the risk of belaboring a point I have developed at length in other places, these practices require the intervention of various deities. Since Genesis 1 effectively vaporizes the very existence of pagan deities, these practices, by definition, cannot have any intrinsic effectiveness. This

---

1   For a more detailed discussion, see J. S. Wright and K. A. Kitchen, "Magic and Sorcery," in *The New Bible Dictionary* (Grand Rapids, MI: Eerdmans, 1962), 766-772.

2   See also Lev. 20:27; 2 Kings 9:22: Is. 8:19; 3:18-23; Jer. 27:9, 10; Ezek. 13:18.

assumption is confirmed by, among others, Isaiah and Jeremiah's satiric and dismissive attitudes towards idols (see Is. 44:9 and Jer. 10:8). The issue is not whether these practices reflect actual powers. They don't. The real problem is linked to loyalty. There is more to engaging in these practices than the actual rituals themselves; participation in these practices signaled a shift in worldview. Deuteronomy 18:13 makes that point clear: "*You must remain completely loyal to the LORD your God.*"

2. Dreams and Visions

Ancient Egyptians and Mesopotamians believed it was possible to seek divine guidance through dreams and visions.[3] The Old Testament does occasionally refer to this mode of revelation. Two of the most notable instances are found in Genesis 41:5-8, 15-16, 25 and Daniel 2:1-23. In Pharaoh's case, the magicians and the wise men are unable to provide an interpretation; only Joseph can. In Nebuchadnezzar's case, the king refuses to divulge the details of the dream, presumably to test the validity of any interpretation that might be offered, but nevertheless demands that his officials interpret the dream. Only Daniel can reveal the details of the dream and offer a valid interpretation. In both cases, this ability to interpret the dreams is not mediated through some sort of ritual, but comes directly from God.

3. The Use of Mandrakes (Gen. 30:14-18)

One could suggest that Rachel attributes magical powers to mandrakes. But as J. S. Wright points out, it is doubtful. Like dill and garlic, plants such as mandrakes were believed to have special properties apart from magic.[4] There is no mention of a ritual or magic formula to accompany the use of mandrakes. It is Yahweh who enables Rachel to have a child (Gen. 30:22).

---

3 For more details, see A. Leo Oppenheim, *The Interpretation of Dreams in the Ancient Near East* (Philadelphia, PA: Ancient Philosophical Society, 1956).

4 Wright, "Magic," 766.

4. Jacob and the Peeled Rods (Gen. 30:37-41)

Jacob's practice in this passage probably reflects a primitive belief in the effect of seen objects on the unborn young. But verse 40 suggests that the results really came about through selective breeding.

5. Samson's Hair (Judg. 16)

The story of Samson's hair appears to support the ancient belief that a man's soul or strength resided in his hair or in some external object. But the narrative makes it clear that Samson's strength derives first and foremost from the power afforded by the Spirit of God, and that only as long as he is faithful to his Nazirite vow.

6. The Power of the Blessing and the Curse

Blessings and curses occurred frequently in the Ancient Near East. We also find them in the Old Testament. Contrary to what many scholars have claimed, most notably R. Kittel,[5] the power of the blessing and the curse does not reside in magic or in the inherent power of the word. In the Ancient Near East, the effectiveness of the blessing and curse formulas derived solely from the intervention of the gods.

Isaac's inability to "recover" the blessing given to Jacob under false pretense (Gen. 27:33, 37) does not reflect some sort of magical belief in the power of the word. There is good evidence to suggest it reflects a legal understanding of the paternal blessing. According to some Nuzi texts, the parental blessing, once given, could not be canceled.[6] This is not a reflection of the word's magical power escaping the speaker, but rather a reflection of the legal status of the promise, which makes such a declaration legally binding.

In Numbers 22, Balak, the king of Zippor, asks Balaam to utter a curse against the people of Israel. But Balaam is unable to follow through on this request, because the word of blessing and the word of cursing depend

---

5   See R. Kittel, "Blessing and Cursing," in *The New Schaff-Herzog Encyclopedia of Religious Knowledge*, ed. S. M Jackson, vol. 2 (New York, NY: Funk and Wagnalis, 1908), 202-203.

6   See C. Gordon, "The Story of Jacob and Laban in the Light of the Nuzi Tablets," BASOR 66 (1937):25-27; _____, "Biblical Customs and the Nuzi Tablets," BA 3 (1940):1-12.

on God' intervention. Their effectiveness is not a function of the inherent power of the word.

7. The Exodus Narrative and the Egyptian Magicians
    The Exodus narrative presents two distinct issues: the power of Moses's staff and the apparent wizardry of the Egyptian magicians.
    There is first the matter of Moses's staff, which God says would be used to perform signs (Exod. 4:17). Strictly speaking, the "signs" performed by Moses's staff are not reflective of magic as such. There is no allusion to a ritual or a magic formula. Moses and Aaron's miraculous interventions depend entirely on God's intervention.
    In regards to the magicians, the Egyptian priests practiced a form of magic that used a combination of traditional ancient Near Eastern rituals and illusionist techniques. The snake/stick sign Moses performs was similar to a trick commonly used by Egyptian magicians. The feat required a cobra. The technique consisted in applying pressure on the muscles at the nape of the neck. As long as the snake was held in this fashion, it created the illusion of rigidity until it was released, at which point, it "turned back" into a snake.[7]
    This is what appears to be happening in Exodus 7:12. The difference is that Aaron had a real staff that actually turned into a snake and vice versa (Exod. 7:19). Aaron's staff is described as "swallowing" the magicians' staffs, demonstrating the overwhelming power of Yahweh.
    We later read that the magicians can imitate some of the actions Moses and Aaron perform. They also have the ability to change water into "blood," but nothing is said about the scale of this conversion. We have to assume it was on a much smaller scale, as Moses had already fouled up the whole land. In Exod. 8:7, we read that magicians can reproduce the plague of the frogs, but the implication is that while they can imitate Moses's feat, there are two caveats. First, the magicians perform this action on a limited scale. Second, they can't reverse the plague initiated by Moses.
    The narrative signals that the magicians quickly reach the bottom of their bag of tricks with the plague of gnats in 8:18-19. First, we note

---

7 See L. Keimer, *Histoires de serpents dans l'Égypte ancienne et moderne* (Cairo, 1947), 16-17

that the magicians have no way of producing the same results. Second, they themselves admit there is something different going on here: *"This is the finger of God,"* acknowledging a qualitative difference between their actions and those of Moses. From that point on, the Egyptian officials are portrayed as powerless before the power of Moses. This story suggests that the magicians had access to a number of "magical" techniques but had no real supernatural powers at their disposal.

8. Samuel's Secret Knowledge (1 Sam. 9:3-6, 15-20)

In 1 Samuel 9, the prophet is portrayed as a seer comparable to the ancient Mesopotamian diviners.[8] Though the narrative describes a practice that parallels the art of divining, Samuel's knowledge is not mediated through some magical ritual; it comes from God himself.

9. The Witch of Endor (1 Sam. 28:3-25).

The narrative involving Saul and the witch of Endor appears at first glance to confirm the reality of psychic phenomena such as summoning of the dead.

The incident involves King Saul who, near the end of his reign, is in dire need of guidance from the Lord as he faces the Philistine army. But Samuel is dead and God remains silent. In desperation, Saul decides, under false pretense, to consult a medium, the witch of Endor, to arouse Samuel from the dead. At first, the witch is extremely reluctant to accommodate the request, fearing this is a trap. She relents, agrees to the request and the prophet appears!

While this text seems to provide a straightforward confirmation of an occult phenomenon, there are a number of factors to consider. First, there is no explicit mention of the witch actually summoning the spirit of Samuel; he just appears. It may be that the summoning act is assumed and its mention superfluous for the story. However, the abrupt transition to the sudden appearance of Samuel remains peculiar. Second, the witch

---

8 For a detailed discussion of prophecy in the Ancient Near East, see H. B. Huffmon, "Prophecy. Ancient Near Eastern Prophecy," in *The Anchor Bible Dictionary*, vol. 5 (New York, NY: Doubleday, 1992), 477-482.

expresses great surprise at the sight of Samuel: "*When the woman saw Samuel, she cried out with a loud voice...*" Why should she be surprised? What did she expect? Presumably, if her powers were real, she would have witnessed such psychic occurrences dozens, perhaps, hundreds of times. The most likely explanation for this unusual reaction is that, for the first time in her "career," she experiences a real vision. A spirit from the dead, literally a divine being (*elohim*), actually appears before her. In conjunction with the distress caused by the vision itself, she would have instantaneously made the connection between this extraordinary event and the real identity of her client, King Saul.[9]

The appearance of Samuel is presented as a real event. The primary cause of this event is not the witch, but God. Samuel's words in verses 16-19 indicate that Saul has become the Lord's mouthpiece to announce his own imminent destruction. Since Samuel is presented explicitly as the Lord's messenger, the implication is that God is the effective agent behind this manifestation, not the witch of Endor.

10. Elijah and the Prophets of Baal (1 Kings 18:15-40)

The well known encounter between Elijah and the prophets of Baal represents a powerful confirmation of the validity of the worldview attested in Genesis 1. In the Ancient Near East, magic is contingent on the intervention of the gods. If, however, there are no gods, as the biblical worldview proclaims, there can be no reality to magical phenomena. Despite the long, arduous and desperate pleas of Baal's prophets, nothing happens. It is only when Elijah prays to God that a miraculous event occurs.

New Testament Passages

1. Condemnation of Magic and Sorcery

As in the Old Testament, the New Testament condemns magic and magical practices. Galatians 5:19-21 lists sorcery as one of the practices Paul qualifies as "works of the flesh." In 2 Timothy 3:1-9, Paul calls Jannes and Jambres, who according to various traditions were two of the magicians who opposed Moses in Egypt,[10] people of "corrupt mind and counterfeit faith"

---

9   See R. W. Klein, *1 Samuel*, Word Biblical Commentary, vol. 10 (Waco, TX: Word Books, 1983), 269.
10   For more details, see A. F. Walls, "Jannes and Jambres," *New Bible Dictionary* (Grand Rapids, MI: Eerdmans, 1962), 599.

who "also oppose the truth." It is important to note that Paul does not highlight the magical powers these men allegedly had, but alludes to their corrupt worldview. In other words, Paul takes the matter out of the magical realm and inserts it back into the realm of reason and ethics. Worshiping demons is linked to idolatry in Revelation 9:20-21. Those who have not been destroyed by plagues are said to have failed to repent from "their sorceries." Revelation 18:23 speaks of the deception brought about by sorcery. In 21:8, the "sorcerers" are among those who are condemned to the "lake that burns with fire" (see Rev. 22:15).

2. Simon the Sorcerer (Acts 8:9-24)

Acts 8 mentions a well known magician named Simon. Simon is renowned as a powerful magician throughout Samaria (vv.10-11). The text reports that Simon became a Christian (v. 13). He began to follow Philip "*and was amazed when he saw the signs and great miracles that took place*"(v.13).

In verse 18, we learn that Simon links the power of the disciples with the laying on of hands and offers to pay to receive this gift: "*Give me also this power so that anyone on whom I lay my hands may receive the Holy Spirit.*" Simon recognizes that the apostles do something that is fundamentally different. In response, Peter curses him (vv. 20-23). Simon's offer indicates a complete misunderstanding of the apostles' ministry and a desire to abduct the power of God to serve his own purposes. Simon's inability to counter Peter's curse suggests that his so-called magical powers are nothing more than parlor tricks.

3. Elymas the Sorcerer (Acts 13:6-12)

Acts 13 refers to a "Jewish sorcerer" known as Elymas or Bar Jesus (v. 6). Luke adds "false prophet," an allusion to the fraudulent character of this man's claims. In response to Elymas's opposition to Barnabas and Paul, Paul rebukes him severely, calling him, among other things, a man "*full of all deceit and villainy....*" (v. 10). Not only does Paul draw attention to the fundamentally deceitful character of Elymas, he demonstrates that Elymas's powers are but quackery and illusion by cursing him blind (vv.11-12).

The Bible and the Demonic

Problematic Old Testament Texts

1. The "Devil/Serpent" and Eve (Gen. 3:1-15)

Christian tradition has consistently seen a manifestation of the devil in the tempting serpent of Genesis 3. While there might be some valid ground to make such an assertion, it is important to note that the devil/serpent is not presented as having the ability to overwhelm its human prey.

The encounter between the serpent and Eve is not akin to a "terrorist attack" with Eve as a powerless victim. The "offensive" is located squarely in the realm of reason. The serpent's statements are straightforward, and Eve has the freedom to respond appropriately. The terms of the temptation are completely transparent. The heart of the issue is whether she will maintain her faith in the integrity of God's Word or whether she will choose to believe the serpent and question the character of God.

2. The "Evil" Spirit from the Lord (1 Sam. 16:13-23; see also 1 Kings 22:6-28)

1 Samuel 16 and 1 Kings 22 respectively allude to an "evil spirit" and a "lying spirit" from the Lord. The immediate question is how God can use an "evil" or "lying" spirit (a demon?) to accomplish his work.

First, in regards to the "evil" spirit of 1 Samuel 16, it must be noted that the Hebrew adjective *ra'* has a broad range of meaning. While it can refer to moral evil (see Gen. 13:13), it can also refer to distress, misery, injury, calamity, curse (see Amos 6:3; Ps. 49:6; Job 2:10).[11]

1 Samuel 16 is set in the context of war. Because Saul has rebelled against Yahweh (see 1 Sam. 15:10.19.22.23), Yahweh has rejected him as king, taking measures to destabilize him. As part of the process to remove Saul from the throne, Yahweh sends a spirit of calamity designed to trouble Saul and undermine his morale. This is not an "evil" spirit, a demon, as such.

As with the preceding case, the "lying spirit" alluded to in 1 Kings 22:22

---

11   For more details, see Francis Brown, *The New Brown—Driver—Briggs—Gesenius Hebrew and English Lexicon* (Lafayette, IN: Associated Publishers and Authors, 1980), 948-949.

occurs in the context of war. It reflects a military strategy designed to feed deceptive information to the enemy in order to misdirect him.

3. The "Satan" in the Book of Job (Job 1:6-2:10)

The prologue of the Book of Job is sometimes used as proof that Satan is a powerful supernatural being with the ability to wreak havoc in a person's life.

At the start, we need to address the literary genre of the book. The Book of Job is not, strictly speaking, a historical narrative. It falls into the category of wisdom literature. While the overall story is framed within a period of time that is generally associated with the patriarchal era, and while the character Job may in fact have been based on a historical figure who may well have experienced great losses, the book is not intended to be read primarily as a historical document. As wisdom literature, it more likely uses a real-life incident as a starting point to develop an extensive, reflective work designed to force the reader to engage a theological issue, in this case, idolatry—the tendency to reduce God and reality to simplistic formula.

Besides the matter of genre itself, the main objection to reading the book strictly as a historical narrative are the implications of such a reading. If the book represents an actual historical description of events, this would imply that, for instance, the prologue provides an actual snapshot of reality. In other words, we live in a universe where Satan meets with God and both engage in bets involving innocent human beings. It would also imply that we live in a universe in which God will take the initiative to invite Satanic attacks upon unsuspecting human beings. This portrayal of metaphysical reality as offered in the Book of Job would be completely at odds with Genesis 1-3, a creation narrative expressly designed to provide the basic architecture of a biblical worldview.

The book's prologue presents Job as a *perfect* man (see Job 1:1, 8, 20-22; 2:3, 10), a portrait that Job confirms later on in the dialogs (see Job 31). The story also adopts the approach that it is perfectly acceptable to replace the lost children with new ones. Finally, the word *Satan* is not used as a proper noun, but functions as a title. It literally means *The Adversary* and appears to describe a character needed to set the stage for the story but is effectively eliminated once his role is fulfilled. All these elements can easily be interpreted within the framework of a wisdom "novel," but make very little sense from the perspective of a historical narrative.

In this light, the portrayal of (the) Satan is not designed, from a literary perspective, to provide a theological architecture for understanding the relationship between the demonic and the human spheres, but to offer a narrative context in which to frame the theological argument that follows the prologue.

4. Territorial Spirits (Daniel 10:10-14)

Daniel 10 is often used to support the notion of demonic territoriality. Verses 13 and 14 represent one of the most critical passages in this respect: "*But the prince of the kingdom of Persia opposed me twenty-one days. So Michael, one of the chief princes, came to help me, and I left him there with the prince of the kingdom of Persia, and have come to help you understand what is to happen to your people at the end of days. For there is a further vision for those days.*"

There is in actuality very little in this passage to support the highly sophisticated concept of demonic territoriality as presented in spiritual warfare literature. Daniel 10 states simply that an unnamed messenger of God was delayed three weeks in delivering a message to Daniel because of the "prince of the kingdom of Persia." This angelic being is finally freed to come to Daniel when Israel's "prince" (v. 21) comes to his aid. This text does not claim to reflect some global demonic network of territorial spirits who systematically oppose the angels of God. It is first and foremost the description of one incident.

There is also the all-important question of literary genre. Some readers may find the constant referencing to genre tiresome, but it is a critically important factor in interpretation. If we really believe that Scripture is inspired and authoritative, we must be equally committed to interpreting Scripture with respect to its literary diversity. In the case of Daniel, we are dealing with apocalyptic literature, a type of literature that has been notoriously difficult to interpret and must be approached with great care.

Apocalyptic language is to a great extent "coded" language used to communicate with an oppressed minority (see Ezekiel and the Book of

Revelation). It is designed to bring encouragement and hope in periods of crisis. The Daniel 10 passage also occurs in the context of a vision (v. 7), which suggests a high degree of symbolism.

Keeping all these factors in mind, it is highly improbable that the intent of this passage is to provide a systematic portrait of demonic territoriality and warfare. It more likely represents a symbolic reference to the political instability that prevails in the world and its impact on the exilic community. This text is addressed to an oppressed people praying for deliverance and asking, as Daniel does throughout his long prayer in chapter 9, why God seems to delay his intervention.

The angel's response communicates three important ideas. First, it provides a message of reassurance to Daniel and the people: God has heard their prayers. Second, it provides a concise explanation of God's timing in bringing deliverance to his people. There are conditions that must be in place before God can complete the various phases of his project. Third, the messenger's emphasis on Daniel's value (vv. 11, 18) is a way to reassure not only Daniel, but also those who read the book, that they have great value in God's eyes. Although God works in history and must sometimes wait out the progression of history to intervene dramatically, the fact remains that God passionately loves his people. Any delay should not be interpreted as a lack of interest on God's part.

The allusion to the conflict between the *"prince of the kingdom of Persia,"* Michael and the unnamed messenger should be read as a metaphor representing the reality of the various forces that oppose God's project and their impact on how God intervenes in human affairs.

Finally, the fact remains that it requires an extraordinary leap of imagination to move from this isolated text to the articulation of a spiritual world populated by a hierarchy of territorial demons.

Problematic New Testament Texts

1. The Healing of Two Demon-Possessed Men (Matt. 8:28-34; see also Luke 8:26-29)

This account is a close parallel to the story of the demon-possessed man found in Mark 5 and discussed in Chapter 3.

2. "The Strong Man" (Matt. 12:24-30; see Mark 3:22-27; Luke 11:15-22)

The Matthew passage is often used to legitimize the practice of "tying the strong man" (Matt. 12:29) during an exorcism. This stems from the belief that the demon must be "neutralized" before he can be cast out. Commentators generally identify the "strong man" as Satan. That may well be the case, but the intent of the text is not to offer precise information about Satan per se.

The "strong man" image is offered as an analogy to explain further why the Pharisees' contention that Jesus is casting out demons by the power of Beelzebub is absurd. Jesus is basically debunking the ridiculous theory that he is doing all these miracles by the power of Satan. In order to make his point, Jesus uses the image of a house invasion. To successfully steal from the house, the owner must be neutralized. Jesus is not trying to teach that Satan must somehow be "bound." The point is that, in the same way a robber cannot count on the homeowner's cooperation, Satan cannot be expected to be co-opted in facilitating the invasion of his own realm. Jesus is casting demons out by the power of the Spirit and his power to do so is overwhelming. [12]

3. The "Stubborn" Evil Spirit (Mark 9:14-32; see also Matt. 17:14-20; Luke 9:37-42)

In this passage, Mark relates the case of a demon the disciples were powerless to cast out (v. 28). This case seems to suggest, by both the inability of the disciples to cast the demon out and Jesus' suggestion that such demons only come out by "prayer" (v. 29), that some demons are particularly "resilient," requiring a more elaborate exorcism ritual.

Though there is a significant degree of drama that accompanies this exorcism,[13] the demon quickly departs the boy at Jesus' command.

The inability of the disciples to expel this demon is at first puzzling.

---

12   See for instance, R. B. Gardner, *Matthew*, Believers Church Bible Commentary (Scottdale, PA: Herald Press, 1991), p. 201; Donald A. Hagner, *Matthew 1-13*, Word Biblical Commentary (Word Books, 1993), p. 344; Thomas C. Long, *Matthew*, Westminster Bible Companion (Westminster John Knox Press, 1997), p. 139.

13   Matthew omits the physical "exit" signs. He simply states that the demon came out and the boy was healed.

In his response, Jesus focuses on prayer.[14] He emphasizes the fact that he did not resort to a complex exorcism procedure. The implication of Jesus' response is that the disciples may have relapsed and used common exorcism techniques rather than simple faith to cast out this particular demon. Tim Geddert writes, "Jesus again focuses on the issue of faith. He says that only prayer makes it possible. One wonders what incantations and formulas they may have tried. Jesus says that it does not depend on technique but on prayer and the faith that makes prayer effective." [15]

4. The "Boomerang" Demons (Luke 11:24-26; see also Matt. 12:43-45)

In Luke 11, the evangelist describes the condition of a man who had an "unclean spirit" cast out. The story then describes a restless spirit who can find no other place to settle and returns to the original "house" accompanied by seven other spirits "more evil than itself," placing the man in a worse condition than he was before. This passage is often offered as rationale to include an explicit injunction for the demon to go to "its place" or for the possibility of the demon eventually returning to the person with new reinforcements if adequate measures are not taken. Ed Murphy, in his *The Handbook of Spiritual Warfare*, paints a rather gloomy picture of what can happen if things are not done just right:

> If effective pre-deliverance counseling is short-circuited, the deliverance will usually only be temporary. If the sin handles still remain, the original demons can easily return—with reinforcements (Matt. 12:42-45)! If the original demons are forbidden to return, millions of other "free-floating" demons like them are ready to latch onto the still existing sin handles in the believer's life. [16]

---

14   It should be noted that the addition of "fasting" in some manuscripts does not reflect the best textual evidence. See Bruce M. Metzger, *A Textual Commentary on the Greek New Testament* (United Bible Societies, 1971), 101.

15   Tim Geddert, *Mark*, Believers Church Bible Commentary (Scottdale, PA: Herald Press, 2001), 224. This point is particularly emphasized in Matthew 17:20: *"He said to them, 'Because of your little faith. For truly I tell you, if you have faith the size of a mustard seed, you will say to this mountain, "Move from here to there," and it will move; and nothing will be impossible for you."*

16   See Murphy, *Spiritual Warfare*, 522.

Before we draw firm conclusions on demons from Luke 11 and Matthew 12, there are a number of factors we need to keep in mind. First, this text is presented as a *parable* to support a point Jesus is making. While the parable may in fact draw on common beliefs about demonic behavior (see Tobit 8:3; Baruch 4:35), it is not presented as a historical description.

The critical lesson of Jesus' teaching centers on the unavoidable question of loyalty. This parable is immediately preceded by Jesus' statement relative to the impossibility of remaining neutral in regards to his person: "*Whoever is not with me is against me, and whoever does not gather with me scatters*" (Luke 11:23). Immediately following this passage, Jesus reminds his audience that it is those who hear the word of God and obey who are blessed (Luke 11:28). In Matthew 12, the parable of the returning demons is directly used as a warning against an "evil and adulterous generation" that asks for a "sign" but has really no intention of changing their allegiance.

For Luke and Matthew, the central issue is loyalty. Both texts make it crystal clear that there is no neutral ground when it comes to Christ. Human beings are either subjected to the kingdom or to the forces that resist it. We may get rid of demonic influence but without allegiance to Christ, it's just a matter of time before we may find ourselves in a worse situation. Neither Luke nor Matthew introduce a magical grid. The man's exacerbated condition does not result from the failure to follow some deliverance ritual, but from not accepting the authority of Jesus.

5. The Girl at Philippi (Acts 16:16-21)

Acts 16:16-21 seems to corroborate the notion that some people have the ability of predicting the future. In the New International Version, verse16 reads: "*Once when we were going to the place of prayer, we were met by a slave girl who had a spirit by which she predicted the future. She earned a great deal of money for her owners by fortune-telling.*"

The expression "*...who had a spirit by which she predicted the future,*" does not necessarily imply that she had the factual ability to tell the future. Literally the text states that the girl had a "spirit of divination (*puthona*)." The NRSV renders this verse a little more accurately: "*...we met a slave-girl who had a spirit of divination and brought her owners a great deal of money by fortune-telling.*" Luke is describing someone who earns money as a fortune-teller and is very effective at her trade because of demonic influence.

Once Paul, out of sheer frustration, exorcises the demon (v. 18), it immediately leaves. The girl loses the ability and, presumably also, the will to work as a fortune-teller. As the New Testament often states, and as decent and rational people have always recognized, fortune-telling is an exercise in deception and manipulation.

6. The Seven Sons of Sceva (Acts 19:13-16)

Acts 19 recounts about some Jews casting out demons and trying to use the name of Jesus to do so. In verses 15-16, Luke reports the catastrophic results of such an approach: "*But the evil spirit said to them in reply, 'Jesus I know, and Paul I know; but who are you?' Then the man with the evil spirit leaped on them, mastered them all, and so overpowered them that they fled out of the house naked and wounded.*"

If demons, as I continuously contend throughout this book, are ontologically powerless beings, how could this one demon-possessed man overwhelm those who were trying to exorcise him?

First, it is the man, under the influence of the demon, who overwhelms the sons of Sceva. While demons may have very little power in and of themselves, men who give themselves to their influence can cause great harm to themselves and others. Second, these Jews were using the name of Jesus within the framework of common exorcist techniques. They believed that the name of Jesus somehow had intrinsic magical powers and the invocation of his name would work in a way similar to a magical formula. There is no magical power in the name of Jesus. Those who use it this way will always be disappointed, not because there is no real power in Jesus Christ, but because they insert the name of Jesus into their own worldview rather than allow Jesus to transform it. They are guilty of syncretism.

As this brief survey suggests, the Bible does not offer clear evidence to support the reality of occult powers or some of the more controversial claims made by Third Wave proponents, such as demonic territoriality. In fact, when the biblical passages that are often invoked to support supernatural claims are carefully examined and interpreted in respect to context and literary genre, they consistently confirm the Creation account's portrait of reality. Only God has the effective ability to intervene supernaturally in history.

Bibliography

Alexander, W. M. Menzies. *Demonic Possession in the New Testament*. Edinburgh: T. & T. Clark, 1902.

Alter, R. *The Art of Biblical Narrative*. New York, NY: Basic Books, 1981.

Anderson, Allan. *An Introduction to Pentecostalism*. Cambridge, UK: Cambridge University Press, 2004.

Anderson, Neil. *The Bondage Breaker*. Eugene, OR: Harvest House, 1991.

Anderson, Neil T. and Timothy M Warner. *The Beginner's Guide to Spiritual Warfare*. Ann Arbor, MI: Vine Books, 2000.

Arnold, Clinton. *Ephesians, Power and Magic: The Concept of Power in Ephesians in Light of its Historical Setting*. Society for New Testament Studies Monograph Series 63. Cambridge: Cambridge University Press, 1989.

_____. *Powers of Darkness. Principalities and Powers in Paul's Letters*. Downers Grove, IL: InterVarsity Press, 1992.

_____. "The 'Exorcism' of Ephesians 6:12 in Recent Research: A Critique of Wesley Carr's View of the Role of Evil Powers in First Century AD Belief." *Journal for the Study of the New Testament* 30 (1987):71-87.

_____. *Three Crucial Questions about Spiritual Warfare*. Grand Rapids, MI: Baker Books, 1997.

Bardsley, Marilyn. "Paul Bernardo and Karla Homolka," Crime Library. http://www.crimelibrary.com/serials/bernardo/bernmain.htm (accessed November 21, 2004).

Barkman, Doug. "Deliver Us from Evil." *Mennonite Brethren Herald* 37 (1998):4-6.

Benoit, Pierre. "Pauline Angelology and Demonology: Reflexions on Designations of Heavenly Powers and on Origin of Angelic Evil According to Paul." *Religious Studies Bulletin* 3 (1983):1-18.

Bean, Matt. "Seeing the Future—or Just Dollar Signs," Court TV.com. http://www.courttv.com/news/feature/misscleo_ctv.html (accessed January 5, 2006).

Berkhof, Hendrikus. *Christ and the Powers*. Scottsdale, PA: Herald Press, 1962 (1953).

Betz, H. D. "Introduction to the Greek Magical Papyri." *The Greek Magical Papyri in Translation*, edited by H. D. Betz, xli-lvi. Chicago, IL: University of Chicago Press, 1986.

Beuken, Willem A. M. "The Human Person in the Vision of Genesis 1-3: A Synthesis of Contemporary Insights." in *Louvain Studies* 24 (1999):3-20.

Bietenhard, Hans. "daimo,nion." in *The New International Dictionary of New Testament Theology*. Vol. 1. ed. by Colin Brown et al, 453-454. Grand Rapids, MI: Zondervan, 1975.

Blocher, Henri. *Original Sin*. New Studies in Biblical Theology. Grand Rapids, MI: Eerdmans, 1999.

Bottéro, Jean. *La plus vieille religion en Mésopotamie*. Folio/histoire. Paris: Gamillard, 1998.

_____. "Le Dieu de la bible." in *La plus belle histoire de Dieu: Qui est le Dieu de la bible?* Paris: Seuil, 1997.

_____. *Naissance de Dieu: la Bible et l'historien*. Paris: Gallimard, 1986.

_____. *Religion in Ancient Mesopotamia*. Tr. Teresa Lavender Fagan. Chicago, IL: The University of Chicago Press, 2001.

Boyd, Greg. *God at War: The Bible and Spiritual Conflict*. Downers Grove, IL: InterVarsity Press, 1997.

_____. *Satan and the Problem of Evil*. Downers Grove, IL: InterVarsity Press, 2001.

Breuninger, Christian. "Where Angels Fear to Tread. Appraising the Current Fascination with Spiritual Warfare." *Covenant Quarterly* 53 (1995):37-43.

Bruce, F. F. *I & II Corinthians*. The New Century Bible Commentary. Grand Rapids, MI: Eerdmans, 1971.

Brueggemann, Walter. *Genesis*. Atlanta, GA: John Knox Press, 1982.

_____. *In Man We Trust*. Richmond, VA: John Knox Press, 1972.

Bubeck, Mark I. *Overcoming the Adversary*. Chicago, IL: Moody, 1984.

Buber, Martin. *Good and Evil*. New York, NY: Scribners Sons, 1952.

_____. *The Adversary*. Chicago, IL: Moody, 1975.

Bufford, Rodger K. *Counseling and the Demonic*. Resources for Christian Counseling. Vol. 17. Dallas, TX: Word Books, 1988.

Burnside, Scott and Alan Cairns. *Deadly Innocence: The True Story of Paul Bernardo, Karla Homolka, and the Schoolgirl Murders*. New York, NY: Warner Books, 1995.

Caird, G. B. *Principalities and Powers*. Oxford: The Clarendon Press, 1956.

Campbell, A. F. and M. A. O'Brien. *Sources of the Pentateuch: Texts, Introductions, Annotations*. Minneapolis, MN: Fortress, 1993.

Carr, Wesley. *Angels and Principalities: The Background, Meaning, and Development of the Pauline Phrase Hai Archai Kai Hai Exousiai*. Society for New Testament Studies Monograph Series 42. Cambridge, MA: Cambridge University Press, 1981.

Cassuto, U. *The Documentary Hypothesis and the Composition of the Pentateuch: Eight Lectures*. Tr. I. Abrahams. Jerusalem: Magnes, 1961.

CNN.com, "Newspaper editorialists fumed in Toronto but largely yawned in Montreal." http://www.cnn.com/2005/WORLD/americas/12/26/canada.swingers.reut/ (accessed January 2, 2006).

Conzelmann, H. *1 Corinthians*. Hermeneia. Philadelphia, PA: Fortress Press, 1975.

Cortes, Juan B. and Florence M. Gatti. *The Case Against Possessions and Exorcisms: A Historical, Biblical, and Psychological Analysis of Demons, Devils, and Demoniacs*. New York, NY: Vantage Press, 1975.

Crawford, T. G. *Blessing and Curse in Syro-Palestinian Inscriptions of the Iron Age*. AUS Series 7 TR. Vol. 120. New York, NY: Peter Lang, 1992.

Cuneo, Michael. *American Exorcisms: Expelling Demons in the Land of Plenty*. Garden City, York, NY: Doubleday, 2001.

Dalbey, Gordon. "When Members Get Caught in The Occult." *Leadership* (Fall Quarter 1989):62-64.

Dalley, Stephanie. *Myths from Mesopotamia*. Oxford: Oxford University Press, 1989.

Dawson, John. *Taking Our Cities for God*. Lake Mary, FL: Creation House, 1989.

Dickason, C. Fred. *Angels, Elect and Evil*. Chicago, IL: Moody Press, 1975.

_____. *Demon Possession and the Christian*. Wheaton, IL: Crossway, 1987.

Ebon, Martin. *The Devil's Bride. Exorcism: Past and Present*. New York, NY: Harper & Row, 1974.

Ediger, Gerald. "Strategic-Level Spiritual Warfare in Historical Retrospect." *Direction* 29 (2000):125-141.

Eller, Vernard. *Christian Anarchy: Jesus' Primacy Over the Powers*. Grand Rapids, MI: Eerdmans, 1987.

Emmerson, R. K. *Antichrist in the Middle Ages: A Study of Medieval Apocalypticism, Art, and Literature*. Seattle, WA: University of Washington Press, 1981.

Evans, Anthony T. *The Battle is the Lord's*. Chicago, IL: Moody Press, 1998.

Faivre, Antoine. "What is Occultism?" In *Hidden Truths. Magic, Alchemy, and the Occult*, ed. by Lawrence E. Sullivan, 3-96. New York, NY: MacMillan, 1989 (1987).

"Family Inheritance: Generational Curses," http://www.demonpossession.com/inheritance.html (accessed September 25, 2002).

Ferguson, Everett. *Demonology of the Early Christian World*. Symposium Series. Vol. 12. New York, NY: Edwin Mellen Press, 1985.

Foerster, Werner. "dai,mwn, daimo,nion, daimoni,zomai, daimoniw,dhj, desidai,mwn, deisidaimoni,a." Vol. 2. in *The Theological Dictionary of the New Testament*. Ed. by Gerhard Kittle et al, 1-19. Grand Rapids, MI: Eerdmans, 1964.

Forsyth, Neil. *The Old Enemy: Satan and the Combat Myth*. Princeton, NJ: Princeton University Press, 1987.

Foster, K. Neill and Paul L. King. *Binding and Loosing: Exercising Authority over Dark Powers*. Camp Hill, PA: Christian Publications, 1998.

Frankl, Viktor E. *Man's Search for Meaning*. Rev. ed. New York, NY: Pocket Books, 1963 (1959).

Friedman, Philip, ed. *Martyrs and Fighters: The Epic of the Warsaw Ghetto.* New York, NY: Praeger, 1954.

Friesen, Randy. "Equipping Principles for Spiritual Warfare." *Direction* 29 (2000):142-152.

Gardner, R. B. *Matthew.* Believers Church Bible Commentary. Scottdale, PA: Herald Press, 1991.

Garrett, D. *Rethinking Genesis: The Sources and Authorship of the First Book of the Pentateuch.* Grand Rapids, MI: Baker, 1991.

Gay, Volney P. *Understanding the Occult.* Minneapolis, MN: Fortress, 1989.

Geddert, Tim. "Demonization: A Biblical View." *The Christian Leader* (February 1996):4-6.

_____. *Mark.* Believers Church Bible Commentary. Scottdale, PA: Herald Press, 2001.

Gerhardsson, B. *The Testing of God's Son.* Tr. J. Toy. Coniectanea Biblica. New Testament, No. 2: fascicle 1. Lund: Gleerup, 1966.

Gilbert, Pierre. *Le motif imprécatoire chez les prophètes bibliques du 8è siècle A.C. à la lumière du Proche-orient ancien,* unpublished doctoral dissertation [Université de Montréal, 1993.

_____. "The Third Wave Worldview: A Biblical Critique." *Direction* 29 (2000):153-168.

Girard René. *Deceit, Desire and the Novel: Self and Other in Literary Structure.* Tr. Y. Freccero. Baltimore, MD: Johns Hopkins University Press, 1965.

_____. *Des choses cachées depuis la fondation du monde.* Bernard Grasset, 1978.

_____. *La violence et le sacré.* Paris: Grasset, 1972.

_____. *Le bouc émissaire.* Paris: Grasset, 1982.

_____. *Violence and the Sacred.* Tr. P. Gregory. Baltimore, MD: Johns Hopkins University Press, 1977.

_____. *The Scapegoat.* Tr. Y. Freccero. Baltimore, MD: Johns Hopkins University Press, 1989.

Gordon, C. "Biblical Customs and the Nuzi Tablets," *Biblical Archeologist* 3 (1940):1-12.

_____. "The Story of Jacob and Laban in the Light of the Nuzi Tablets." *Bulletin of the American Schools of Oriental Research* 66 (1937):25-27.

Green, Michael. *I Believe in Satan's Downfall.* London: Hodder & Stoughton, 1981.

Grenz, Stanley J. "Superstition: A Christian Perspective," *The Asia Journal of Theology.* Vol. 8 (1994): 365-378.

Guelich, Robert A. *Mark 1-8:26.* Word Biblical Commentary. Vol. 34A. Dallas, TX: Word, 1989.

Hagner, Donald A. *Matthew 1-13.* Word Biblical Commentary. Vol. 33a. Word Books, 1993.

Hamilton, Victor P. *The Book of Genesis: Chapters 1-17.* New International Commentary on the Old Testament. Grand Rapids, MI: Eerdmans, 1990.

Hammond, Frank and Ida. *Pigs in the Parlor. A Practical Guide to Deliverance.* Kirwood, MO: Impact Christian Books, 1973.

_____. *The Breaking of Curses.* Spiritual Warfare Series. Vol. 5. Kirwood, MO: Impact Christian Books, 1993.

Hart, Archibald. "Regeneration, Deliverance or Therapy?" in *Leadership* (Summer Quarter (1991):72-79.

Hasel, Gerhard F. "The Polemic Nature of the Genesis Cosmology." *The Evangelical Quarterly* 46 (1974):81-102.

_____. *I Believe in Satan's Downfall.* Grand Rapids, MI: Eerdmans, 1981.

Hiebert, Paul G. "Biblical Perspectives on Spiritual Warfare." In *Anthropological Reflections on Missiological Issues,* 203-215. Grand Rapids, MI: Baker Books, 1994.

_____. "The Flaw of the Excluded Middle." In *Anthropological Reflections on Missiological Issues,* 189-201. Grand Rapids, MI: Baker Books, 1994.

_____. "Healing and the Kingdom." In *Anthropological Reflections on Missiological Issues,* 217-253. Grand Rapids, MI: Baker Books, 1994.

_____. "Spiritual Warfare and Worldviews." *Direction* 29 (2000):114-124.

_____. "Spiritual Warfare and Worldviews." *Evangelical Review of Theology* 24 (2000):240-256.

Hollenbach, Paul W. "Jesus, Demoniacs, and Public Authorities." *Journal of the American Academy of Religion* 49 (1981):567-88.

Hollenweger, W. J. *The Pentecostals: The Charismatic Movement in the Churches.* Tr. R. A. Wilson. Minneapolis, MN: Augsburg, 1972 [1969].

Horrobin, Peter. *Healing Through Deliverance: The Biblical Basis.* Chichester, England: Sovereign World, 1991.

Howard, J. Keir. "New Testament Exorcism and its Significance Today." *The Expository Times* 96 (1985):105-109.

Huffmon, H. B. "Prophecy. Ancient Near Eastern Prophecy." In *The Anchor Bible Dictionary,* edited by D. N. Freedman, 477-482. Vol. 5. New York, NY: Doubleday, 1992.

Israel, Martin. *Exorcism. The Removal of Evil Influences.* London: SPCK, 1997.

Jacobs, Donald R. *Demons: An Examination of Demons at Work in the World Today.* Scottdale, PA: Herald, 1976.

Jacobsen, Thorkild. "Mesopotamian religion." *Encyclopædia Britannica Online.* http://www.britannica.com/eb/article-68282 (accessed September 27, 2007).

James Randi Educational Foundation. http://www.randi.org/.

Johns, Loren L. and James R. Krabill, eds. *Even the Demons Submit.* Occasional Papers, No. 25. Elkhart, IN: Institute of Mennonite Studies, 2006.

Kaiser, Christopher. *Creation and the History of Science.* London: Marshall Pickering, 1991.

Kaufmann, Yehezkel. *The Religion of Israel: From Its Beginnings to the Babylonian Exile.* Chicago, IL: University of Chicago Press, 1960.

Kee, Howard. *Medicine, Miracle and Magic in New Testament Times.* SNTSMS. Vol. 55. Cambridge, England: Cambridge University Press, 1986.

Keimer, L. *Histoires de serpents dans L'Egypte ancienne et moderne.* Cairo, 1947.

Kelly, Henry Ansgar. *The Devil at Baptism: Ritual, Theology, and Drama.* Ithaca, NY: Cornell Univ. Press, 1984.

Kirk, G. S. *Myth: Its Meaning and Functions in Ancient and Other Cultures.* Cambridge, England: Cambridge University Press, 1970.

Kittel, R. "Blessing and Cursing." In *The New Schaff-Herzog Encyclopedia of Religious Knowledge,* edited by S. M. Jackson, 202-203. Vol. 2. New York, NY: Funk and Wagnalis, 1908.

Klein, R. W. *1 Samuel.* Word Biblical Commentary. Vol. 10. Waco, TX: Word Books, 1983.

Koch, Kurt. *Between Christ and Satan.* Grand Rapids, MI: Kregel, 1971.

_____. *Christian Counseling and Occultism.* Grand Rapids, MI: Kregel, 1972.

_____. *Demonology: Past and Present.* Grand Rapids, MI: Kregel, 1973.

_____. *The Devil's Alphabet.* Grand Rapids, MI: Kregel, 1969.

_____. *Occult Bondage and Deliverance.* Grand Rapids, MI: Kregel, 1971.

_____. *Occult ABC.* Grand Rapids, MI.: Kregel, 1981.

König, A. *Here Am I: A Believer's Reflection on God.* Grand Rapids, MI: Eerdmans, 1982.

Kraft, Charles H. *Christianity with Power: Your Worldview and Your Experience of the Supernatural.* Ann Arbor, MI: Vine Books, 1989.

_____. *Defeating Dark Angels.* Ann Arbor, MI: Vine Books, 1992.

Kyle, Richard. *The New Age Movement in American Culture.* University Press of America, 1995.

_____. "The Occult Roars Back: Its Modern Resurgence." *Direction* 29 (2000):91-99.

_____. *The Religious Fringe: A History of Alternative Religions in America.* Downers Grove, IL: InterVarsity Press, 1993.

Lane, Anthony N. S., ed. *The Unseen World: Christian Reflections on Angels, Demons, and the Heavenly Realm.* Grand Rapids, MI: Baker Books, 1996.

Lawson, Steven. "Defeating Territorial Spirits." In *Engaging the Enemy*, 29-41. Ventura, CA: Regal, 1991.

Lea, Larry. "Binding the Strong Man." In *Engaging the Enemy*, 83-95. Ventura, CA: Regal, 1991.

Lewis, C. S. *Mere Christianity.* New York, NY: HarperSanFrancisco, 2001.

_____. *Miracles.* New York, NY: Macmillan, 1947.

_____. *The Problem of Pain.* New York, NY: HarperSanFrancisco, 1996 (1940).

Loewen, Jacob. "Demon Possession and Exorcism in Africa, in the New Testament Context and in North America," In *Essays on Spiritual Bondage and Deliverance, Occasional Papers No. 11*, edited by William M. Swartley, 118-145. Elkhart, IN: Institute of Mennonite Studies, 1988.

Lowe, Chuck. "Do Demons Have Zip Codes?" *Christianity Today* (July 13, 1998):57.

_____. *Territorial Spirits and World Evangelisation?* Ross-Shire, Scotland: Christian Focus, 1998.

Maier, G. "How did Moses Compose the Pentateuch?" *Stulos Theological Journal.* Vol. 1 (1993):157-161.

Martens, Elmer. *God's Design: A Focus on Old Testament Theology.* 3rd ed. N. Richland Hills, TX: Bibal, 1998 (1981).

Matheson, Roy. "When you're in the War Zone." *Christian Counseling Today* (Winter 1994):20-24.

Matthews, Victor H. and Don C. Benjamin. *Old Testament Parallels.* 2nd ed. New York/Mahwah, NJ: Paulist Press, 1997 (1991).

Mauser, U. W. *Christ in the Wilderness. Studies in Biblical Theology.* 1st series, No. 39. London: SCM, 1963.

McAlpine, Thomas H. *Facing the Powers? Innovations in Mission.* Monrovia, CA: MARC, 1991.

McCall, Kenneth. *Healing the Family Tree*. London: Sheldon Press, 1982.

Metzger, Bruce M. *A Textual Commentary on the Greek New Testament*. United Bible Societies, 1971.

Miller, Paul M. *The Devil Did Not Make Me Do It: A Study in Christian Deliverance*. Scottdale, PA: Herald, 1977

Montgomery, John W., ed. *Demon Possession*. Minneapolis, MN: Bethany House, 1976.

_____. *Principalities and Powers: The World of the Occult*. Minneapolis, MN: Bethany Fellowship, 1973.

Moreau, A. Scott. *Essentials of Spiritual Warfare*. Wheaton, IL: Harold Shaw, 1997.

Murphy, Ed. *The Handbook for Spiritual Warfare*. Nashville, TN: Thomas Nelson, 1992.

Newport, John P. *The New Age Movement and the Biblical Worldview*. Grand Rapids, MI: Eerdmans, 1998.

Noll, Stephen F. *Angels of Light, Powers of Darkness*. Downers Grove, IL: InterVarsity Press, 1998.

North, Gary. *Unholy Spirits.: Occultism and New Age Humanism*. Fort Worth, TX: Dominion Press, 1986.

Nugent, Christopher. *Masks of Satan: The Demonic in History*. London: Sheed and Ward, 1983.

Olson, Ken. *Exorcism: Fact or Fiction*. Nashville, TN: Thomas Nelson, 1992.

Oppenheim, Leo A. *Ancient Mesopotamia*. Rev. ed. Chicago, IL: The University of Chicago Press, 1977 (1964).

Osborne, Grant. *The Hermeneutical Spiral*. Downers Grove, IL: InterVarsity Press, 1991.

Otis, George Jr. *The Twilight Labyrinth*. Grand Rapids, MI: Chosen Books, 1997.

Page, Sydney H. T. *Powers of Evil*. Grand Rapids, MI: Baker Books, 1995.

Pannell, William E. "Evangelism and Power." *International Review of Mission* 69 (1980):49-55

Peck, M. Scott. *People of the Lie: The Hope for Healing Human Evil.* New York, NY: Simon & Schuster Inc., 1983.

Pedersen, J. *Israel. Its Life and Culture.* Vol. 1. London: Oxford University Press, 1926 (1920).

Pelt, M. V.; Kaiser, W. C. and D. I. Block. "x;Wr...." *New International Dictionary of Old Testament Theology and Exegesis,* edited by W. A. VanGemeren, 1073-1078.Vol. 5. Grand Rapids, MI: Zondervan, 1997.

Peretti, Frank E. *This Present Darkness.* Westchester IL: Crossway Books, 1986.

_____. *Piercing the Darkness.* Westchester IL: Crossway Books, 1989.

Perry, Michael, ed. *Deliverance: Psychic Disturbances and Occult Involvement.* 2nd ed. London: SPCK, 1996 [1987].

Peterson, Robert. *Are Demons for Real? Dramatic Incidents of Spirit Phenomena in Conflict with the Power of Christ.* Chicago, IL: Moody Press, 1972.

Philpott, Kent. *A Manual of Demonology and the Occult.* Grand Rapids, MI: Zondervan, 1973.

Powlison, David. *Power Encounters.* Grand Rapids, MI: Baker Books, 1995.

Pron, Nick. *Lethal Marriage. The Unspeakable Crimes of Paul Bernardo and Karla Homolka.* New York, NY: Ballantine Books, 1996.

Rausch, D. *A Legacy of Hatred: Why Christians Must Not Forget the Holocaust* Chicago, IL: Moody, 1984.

Re, Richard. "A Persisting Evil." *Environment.* Vol. 23 (2002). http://hir.harvard.edu/articles/951/1/ (accessed January 20, 2006).

Riley, G. "Demon." In *Dictionary of Deities and Demons in the Bible,* edited by Karel van der Toorn, Bob Becking, and Pieter W. van der Horst, 235-240. Grand Rapids, MI: Eerdmans, 1999.

Ritchie, Mark. *Spirit of the Rainforest.* 2nd ed. Chicago, IL: Island Lake Press, 2000 (1996).

Russell, Jeffrey B. *Lucifer: The Devil in the Middle Ages.* Ithaca, NY: Cornell University Press, 1984.

_____. *Satan: The Early Christian Tradition.* Ithaca, NY: Cornell University Press, 1981.

_____. *The Devil: Perceptions of Evil from Antiquity to Primitive Christianity.* Ithaca, NY: Cornell University Press, 1977.

_____. *Mephistopheles: The Devil in the Modern World.* Ithaca, NY: Cornell University Press, 1986.

Schlier, Heinrich, *Principalities and Powers in the New Testament.* New York, NY: Herder & Herder, 1961.

Shield of Faith Ministries. "Generational Sins and Weaknesses Checklist." http://www.shieldofaith.org/resources/Library/generational_sins_and_weaknesses .htm (accessed September 25, 2002).

Shuster, Marguerite. "Giving the Devil More than His Due." *Leadership* (Summer Quarter 1991):64-67.

_____. *Power, Pathology, Parados: The Dynamics of Evil and Good.* Grand Rapids: Zondervan, 1987.

Sire, James. *The Universe Next Door.* Downers Grove, IL: InterVarsity Press, 1988.

Sterk, Vernon J. "Territorial Spirits and Evangelization in Hostile Environments." In *Engaging the Enemy*, 145-163. Ventura, CA: Regal Books, 1991.

Summers, Montague. *The History of Witchcraft and Demonology.* 2nd ed. New York, NY: University Books, 1956.

Swartley, Willard M. "Biblical Faith Confronting Opposing Spiritual Realities." *Direction* 29 (2000):100-113.

_____, ed. *Essays on Spiritual Bondage and Deliverance.* Occasional Papers, No 11. Elkhart, IN: Institute of Mennonite Studies, 1988.

_____. "Exorcism." In *Mennonite Encyclopedia*, ed. by C. J. Dyck and D. Martin, 285-287. Scottdale, PA: Herald, 1990.

_____. "Satan." In *Mennonite Encyclopedia*, ed. by C. J. Dyck and D. Martin. 791-794. Scottdale, PA: Herald, 1990.

Tennant, Agnieszka. "In Need of Deliverance." *Christianity Today* (Sept. 3, 2001): 46-63

Tinker, Melvin. "The Phantom Menace: Territorial Spirits and SLSW." *Churchman* 114 (2000):71-81.

Twelftree, Graham. *Christ Triumphant: Exorcism Then and Now*. London: Hodder and Stoughton, 1985.

_____. *Jesus the Exorcist*. Peabody, MA: Hendrickson, 1993.

_____. "The Place of Exorcism in Contemporary Ministry." *St. Mark's Review* (September 1986):25-39.

Unger, Merrill F. *Biblical Demonology*. Wheaton, IL: Scripture Press, 1957.

_____. *Demons in The World Today*. Wheaton, IL: Tyndale, 1976.

_____. *What Demons Can Do to Saints*. Chicago, IL: Moody, 1977.

Van der Meer, Erwin. "Reflections on Spiritual Mapping." *Africa Journal of Evangelical Theology* 20 (2001):47-70.

Von Rad, Gerhard. *Genesis*. Rev. ed. Philadelphia, PA: Westminster, 1972 (1961).

Wagner, C. Peter, ed. *Breaking Strongholds in Your City*. Ventura, CA: Regal Books, 1993.

_____. *Confronting the Powers*. Ventura, CA: Regal Books, 1996.

_____, ed. *Engaging the Enemy*. Ventura, CA: Regal Books, 1991.

_____. *How to Have a Healing Ministry without Making Your Church Sick*. Ventura CA: Regal Books, 1988.

_____. *Praying with Power*. Ventura, CA: Regal, 1997.

_____, ed. *Signs and Wonders Today*. Altamonte Springs, FL: Creation House, 1987.

_____. "Territorial Spirits and World Missions." *Evangelical Missions Quarterly* 25 (1989):278-88.

_____. "The Key to Victory is Building the Strong Man." *Ministries Today* (Nov/ Dec. 1986):84.

_____. *The Third Wave of the Holy Spirit.* Ann Arbor MI: Vine Books, 1988.

_____. *Warfare Prayer: How to Seek God's Power and Protection in the Battle to Build His Kingdom.* Ventura, CA: Regal Books, 1992.

Wagner, C. Peter and F. Douglas Pennoyer, eds. *Wrestling with Dark Angels.* Ventura, CA: Regal Books, 1990.

Walls, A. F. "Jannes and Jambres." In *New Bible Dictionary*, edited by J. D. Douglas, 599. Grand Rapids, MI: Eerdmans, 1962.

Warner, Timothy M. *Spiritual Warfare.* Wheaton, IL: Crossway, 1991.

Wenham, Gordon J. *Genesis 1-15, Word Biblical Commentary.* Vol. 1. Waco, Texas: Word 1987.

Westermann, Claus. *Creation.* Fortress Press, 1974.

_____. *Genesis 1-11.* Tr. John J. Scullion. Minneapolis, MN: Augsburg 1984 (1974).

White, John. *When the Spirit Comes with Power.* Downers Grove, IL: InterVarsity Press, 1988.

_____. *The Devil: What the Scriptures Teach about Him.* Wheaton, IL: Tyndale, 1971.

White, Thomas B. *The Believer's Guide to Spiritual Warfare.* Ann Arbor, MI: Vine, 1990.

_____. *Breaking Strongholds.* Ann Arbor, MI: Vine, 1993.

Williams, Stephen. *Invisible Darkness.* Bantam, 1997.

Wilmoth, Joe D. "After Deliverance, Then What? *Leadership* (Summer Quarter 1991): 68-70.

Wimber, John. *Power Evangelism: Signs and Wonders Today.* Toronto, ON: Hodder and Stoughton, 1985.

Wink, Walter. *Engaging the Powers.* Minneapolis, MN: Fortress, 1992.

_____. *Naming the Powers: The Language of Power in the New Testament.* Philadelphia, PA: Fortress, 1984.

_____. *The Powers That Be.* Garden City, NY: Doubleday, 1998.

_____. *Unmasking the Powers.* Philadelphia, PA: Fortress, 1986.

_____. *Violence and Nonviolence in South Africa: Jesus' Third Way.* Philadelphia, PA: New Society Publishers, 1987.

Wright, J. S. and K. A. Kitchen. "Magic and Sorcery." In *The New Bible Dictionary*, edited by J. D. Douglas, 766-772. Grand Rapids, MI: Eerdmans, 1962.

Yoder, John Howard. *The Politics of Jesus.* Grand Rapids, MI: Eerdmans, 1972.

_____. *What Would You Do? A Serious Answer to a Standard Question.* Scottdale, PA: Herald, 1983.